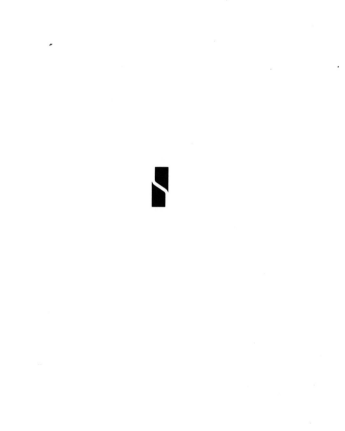

Errors, Lies, and Libel

Peter E. Kane

With a Foreword by Elmer Gertz

Southern Illinois University Press
Carbondale and Edwardsville

Printed in the United States of America

Edited and designed by Mary A. Rohrer
Production supervised by Natalia Nadraga

95   94   93   92   4   3   2   1

Library of Congress Cataloging-in-Publication Data

Kane, Peter E., 1932–
  Errors, lies, and libel/Peter E. Kane.
     p.   cm.
  Includes bibliographical references (p.   ).
  1. Trials (Libel)—United States.   2. Libel and slander—
United States.   I. Title.
KF221.L5K36   1992
345.73'0256—dc20
[347.305256]   90-25032
   ISBN 0-8093-1719-2. — ISBN 0-8093-1720-6 (pbk.)   CIP

The paper used in this publication meets the minimum
requirements of American National Standard for
Information Sciences—Permanence of Paper for
Printed Library Materials, ANSI Z39.48-1984. ∞

Contents

Contents

Foreword

As the protagonist in one of the two leading libel cases, I feel a sort of parental pride and responsibility for the development of a law with respect to defamation. This book, therefore, has a special interest for me. It will hold the interest of others as well, including those who have not personally been involved in litigation.

I like its emphasis on actual trials, rather than exclusively on the reports of appellate reviews. Judge Jerome Frank, one of the most profound students of the law, used to say that schools that purported to teach only through reported cases shortchanged students. He claimed that students would absorb much more of the reality of their intended profession if they poured over transcripts of trials, discovery proceedings, motions, and the like. That is the basis on which I have written my definitive account of my own landmark case, and it is the basis on which the author of this book proceeded.

Peter Kane has not only explained the constitutional guidelines that have evolved since 1964 when *New York Times v. Sullivan* was decided by the Supreme Court, but also explained the Court's continual refining and redefining of the relevant law. We are like spectators, or even participants, in an absorbing human drama in which real people are pitted against each other, with results that are often painful, sometimes pleasant.

Wars and civil strife are the bloody background of many of the cases. We live through Dr. Martin Luther King's historical effort to overcome the bondage of his people. We fight fruitlessly in Vietnam. As in my case, we contend against the extremism of the Far Right and rejoice when reason appears to triumph, if only for the moment.

Were it not for the *Sullivan* ruling, the civil rights movement might have been set back for years. Were it not for the *Sullivan* ruling, libel law would not have advanced so rapidly, and there would have been fewer ups and downs in the law.

The law of libel has not yet reached its outer limits. It is still being fashioned by a high court that has changed its membership and with that its vistas. It seems to have embarked on what may be an impossible task, making the constitutional as-

pects of the law, with respect to reputation, absolute, clear, and unmistakable.

The dimensions of the problem are recogniz-
able when one considers libel in the context of another issue with which it is almost inextricably
intertwined—the First Amendment freedoms of
the press and of speech. How can we reasonably
and fairly protect reputation without interfering
unduly with freedom of expression? Although a
difficult problem for some, to Justice Black it was a
relatively simple matter—everything must give
way to freedom of expression. Yet even he demonstrated limited vision, as when he opined in his
dissent in the *Tinker* case that high school students
did not have the right of political protest that their
parents had.

Peter Kane suggests, justifiably in my opinion, that ruined reputations are just as important,
perhaps more so, than broken limbs, and one
must receive recompense when one is harmed,
whatever the cause or consequences. There are
some who are so unconcerned about reputation,
Justice Black for one, that they fail to see why it
must be protected.

Perhaps it is best that the struggle for definition is not completely resolved in our day. After

all, scarcely a generation has passed since the struggle began in 1964 with the *Sullivan* case. We should let the varied cases come before the courts, so they and we may receive the benefits of experience and be enabled to correct errors and misconceptions. We should never forget that the law as it is today arose out of a special situation, the struggle for civil rights. Other special situations may arise.

Why is it that libel cases hold such attraction not only for us in the United States but especially for people in England? Libel cases do not have the dryness of disputes over mere dollars. They are not as circumscribed as struggles over contracts, real estate transactions, zoning, and the like. Real people, real issues, real results are involved, as evinced by the cases in this book.

Even if a case has been decided by the highest court, it is not at an end. In a sense, the dispute is never resolved, because it is too important to be hemmed in by a mere court ruling, even if it is by the highest court. We continue to ask if the decision is right and, if it is wrong, how the injury can be undone.

As you read these pages, they will stir up images of people who battle, bleed, and breed. What impelled them to rise up and protest despite expenditures of time, energy, and funds they often could not afford?

My insightful friend Peter Irons has written a book, *The Courage of Their Convictions*, that gives at least part of the answer. It tells of sixteen persons, myself included, who carried their sometimes desperate fights for their rights to the highest court. Sometimes they won, sometimes they lost, but always they were able to hold their heads high because they did not give up, whatever the cost.

We see here the same kind of persons and their partisans. One general, Sharon, travels across the seas to seek vindication, only to receive it at home rather than abroad. Another general, Westmoreland, faces greater odds in the courts than in the battlefields. Always to them there is one enemy—the media. To others the press is the great conglomerate of heroes, battling for causes and the people. In each of these cases the press figures in some way—as defendant, as forum, as fortress. The press claims greater rights than the ordinary person. Should this be so? As you read about the cases in this volume, your answer may differ from case to case. In any event, you will be interested, entertained, and enlightened.

And you will find that there are related fields of the law. One example is what we sum up as the law of privacy. In some respects privacy arouses a more fiercely emotional response than does libel. We begin to sense that there may be nothing more important than the person, the inner being. It was Walt Whitman who said, "I sing myself." That is what the persons in this array of cases sing.

—Elmer Gertz

Preface

Almost every nation has laws or constitutional provisions that pledge support for freedom of expression. However, in every one of these nations, including the United States of America, freedom of expression is not absolute. Laws and legal interpretations limit the extent of the freedom and provide penalties for violations. Often these limits arise when the principle of freedom of expression appears to conflict with some other social value. For example, the social distress caused by sexually explicit communication leads to laws that restrict what is defined as obscene communication. Unrestrained reporting about a gruesome murder case can be seen as harming a criminal defendant's right to a fair trial.

Another area where these conflicts are marked is that of defamation, the laws and court rulings dealing with the problems of libel and slander. We live in a society that places a high value on an individual's good name and reputation.

Nowhere is that idea more clearly stated than in Proverbs 22:1: "A good name is more to be desired than great riches." Examples of this ancient aphorism in practice abound, but perhaps no current one is more obvious than the lengths to which former President Richard Nixon and members of his administration have gone to prevent public disclosure of documents and tapes of that administration. The issue is not national security; it is rather an effort to salvage as much reputation as possible by concealing as much evidence of malfeasance as possible for as long as possible. The former president is very much concerned about the public's opinion of him and his place in the history books.

In some cases individuals seek to secure both good reputation and great riches by filing defamation suits against those who communicate information considered damaging to a reputation. News stories of multi-million-dollar suits for marginal or doubtful injuries to reputation are not unusual. Massive jury awards in these cases are also not uncommon, expressing a basic concern for the protection of reputation by the general public who make up juries. These awards may also reflect current public hostility toward the news media, hostility which is a result of political attacks on the news media by public figures whose reputations are harmed by the truth. The arrogance too often displayed by people in the news media has also contributed to this hostility.

The goal of this volume is to stimulate critical and creative thinking about the problems of defamation. While it is good to understand the "rules of the game" in this area of media law, effective problem solving requires more. Both the public and media practitioners need greater understanding of these problems to help achieve a proper balance between freedom of expression and protection of reputation.

For those of us interested in the problems of freedom of expression, the most compelling issues usually involve conflicts between competing interests. Such conflicts involve more than understanding a philosophy or the established rules in particular cases. They confront us with legitimate demands based upon real values. Some or all of those demands and their underlying values must be compromised in order to resolve the conflict. Several questions arise. Which interests are to be compromised? How are they to be compromised? What is the rationale for this compromise?

Students of journalism are often exposed to instruction in media law, a major element of which is learning the rules regarding defamation as they have been developed through actual court cases. Most of the time that study of rules and court cases does not include an examination of the real people and the actual conflicts between freedom of expression and protection of reputation that are the heart of the case. In this volume I tell these stories of the actual conflicts and the real people involved. One key to understanding this freedom of expression-protection of reputation conflict is an examination of the actions and apparent motivation of those involved in these conflicts in the courts. What was said about these people, and why and how was it reported? What is the real, or imagined, injury that leads people to sue? Answering these questions enhances our understanding of the legal outcomes of the cases considered here.

Since 1964 the Supreme Court of the United States has considered a substantial number of cases dealing with the conflicts that are at the heart of libel suits. In each case the Court has struggled to arrive at what it believes is the correct compromise. Because each new case builds upon prior decisions and opinions, the major cases considered in this volume are presented in a roughly chronological order with some grouping of cases that deal with similar issues.

Anyone reading about these cases should conclude that our present system for resolving the conflicts between freedom of expression and protection of reputation does not work very well. The rationales for the compromises are shifting. The rules that have grown up and proliferated over the last twenty-five years are not clearly understood by many people. While some criticize these legal rules for being unbalanced in favor of the news media and their freedom to publish even false information, others claim that the rules allow or even encourage meritless suits to harass media with the courage to publish unpleasant truths. Whatever their view about the fairness of the present rules, all interested parties agree that the costs of vindication for all sides in these conflicts are too high. Thus it is not surprising that libel reform is a topic of major interest in the field of media law. The final chapter of this study offers an introduction to some of the current thinking in this area.

This study is designed to focus on the highlights of defamation as this author sees them. For those readers who want more information, an annotated case list and a selected annotated bibliography have been provided. Most of the cases mentioned in this work have court opinions that can be read and reflected upon by those interested.

Time for the initial preparation of this study was made available through a sabbatical leave granted me by the State University of New York. Special thanks is also due my colleague Chad Skaggs who used his outstanding knowledge of libel law and his many years of experience as a reporter and editor to help me say clearly what I intended to say and to explain fully what I had left incomplete or obscure.

Errors,
Lies,
and Libel

1

The Problem

You open your morning newspaper, and there under a front-page headline reading "Accused Child Molester Arrested" are your name and photograph. You have not been either accused or arrested. The paper has made a major mistake in identifying the person accused. You immediately call this mistake to the paper's attention, and the following day in a box on page three under the heading "Correction," the paper admits its error and apologizes for any inconvenience that may have been caused.

As a result of this episode, your life changes significantly. Your friends, neighbors, and associates have all read the original newspaper story. While many may also have read the correction published the next day, suspicion has been planted about your moral character and psychological stability. Although no one says anything directly to you, you perceive the strange looks and feel the changes in attitude that have taken place.

Your good relations with most others have been undermined. Your good name in the community has been severely damaged through absolutely no fault of your own.

In a situation such as this one a common American response is: Sue the bastards! After all, you have received a personal injury just as though you had been hit by a truck. However, before taking action two questions need to be considered. First, do you have grounds for suing, and second, what will you achieve by suing?

To answer the first question it is necessary to know what you would need to prove in this special personal injury action known as a libel suit. Simply stated, five elements need to be shown in a libel suit: (1) publication, (2) identification, (3) defamation, (4) injury, and (5) fault. Publication occurs when the communication at issue is divulged to someone other than you and the communicator. In your case the newspaper divulged the information to the entire community, so publication has taken place. There must be identification of a specific person, and your name and photograph clearly identify you.

The third element of what constitutes defamation is a bit more difficult. To begin with, the

information published about you must be false,
which is the case. However, not all false information is defamatory. Over the years the courts and
the law have determined that some errors do not
provide grounds for a suit. Things such as an incorrect address, middle name, or age are viewed
as harmless errors; so too is an erroneous report of
your death. On the other hand, false reports of
criminal behavior, immoral conduct, or physical or
mental illness are defamatory. In the case at hand
the false report of your alleged criminal conduct,
which also touches on sexual immorality and mental illness, is obviously defamatory.

The last two elements are injury and fault.
The assault on your mental health and good name
as demonstrated by the behavior of those around
you since the report would suggest that there is
evidence of injury. The question of fault is one of
determining what, if any, responsibility the newspaper has for publishing the error. Should it be
held accountable for any mistake? This standard is
called that of *strict liability*. Should it be held responsible only if it did not exercise the care expected of the average prudent person? This is the
negligence standard of fault. Or should the paper
only be responsible if it deliberately lies or shows a

reckless disregard for whether the information is true or false? This standard is given the shorthand label of *malice* even though it has nothing to do with the common meaning of the word *malice*. The courts have decided that different classes of people are required to prove different standards of fault. As a private person you would probably need to prove no more than that the newspaper was negligent in its false identification of you as the person accused of this sex crime.

The question of what may be achieved by a libel suit is a far more difficult one because there is no simple legal formula that can be applied. One motive for suing might be to receive financial compensation for the injury that you received. If hit by a truck, you would expect to be compensated for your medical expenses. You might also seek additional compensation for permanent injuries such as the loss of a finger as well as the pain and suffering that you experienced. The dollar value of pain and suffering is hard to establish and is even more so when that pain and suffering have been caused by another's words rather than by another's careless driving. Also hard to establish is the dollar value of the deterioration in your relations with people who read the publication of the

4

defamation. In sum, if you sue to receive adequate compensation for your injury, how can you determine what that compensation should be?

A strong element in the "sue the bastards" approach to these problems is the desire for revenge. The newspaper's false report has punished you, and now you want to get even by making the paper pay you a large sum. Such an award, called *punitive* damages, is often assessed like the fine that the driver of the truck that hit you might pay for running a red light, but unlike the latter situation involving traffic violations, there is no clear schedule of fines in libel suits. Furthermore, if the newspaper did not knowingly lie or show reckless disregard for the truth or falsehood of what it printed, are punitive damages appropriate? Will the paper be more careful to avoid accidental errors in the future as the result of having to pay a large damage award?

In the final analysis what you probably really want is to have the false accusation removed and your reputation and peace of mind restored. But are these obtainable goals? Can anything realistically be done to restore everything to the way it was before the false report was published? The newspaper tried to rectify the situation through its prompt publication of a retraction and apology, but even this was inadequate. How will a financial award make things any different? On the one hand it can be argued that such an award will really make no difference, leading to the conclusion that a libel suit should not be pursued. On the other hand a public trial, particularly one that results in a substantial judgment against the newspaper, might well be widely reported and serve as a form of public vindication and restoration of your reputation. Those who were unsure may well be persuaded by such a judgment that the accusation was indeed false. From this point of view a libel suit must be pursued.

The foregoing fictional example provides an introduction to the perplexing problem of libel in the United States, where society places a high value on both freedom of expression and personal reputation. Although the constitutional guarantee clearly pledges that there will be "no law abridging freedom of . . . the press," legislatures and the courts have always recognized that the laws of defamation (the broad term for libel) and the suits that they allow are exceptions to the freedom of the press guarantee. The press (the term used here generically to cover all media of mass communication) is not free to publish whatever it wants. Punishment can be rendered for the publication of some falsehoods (the root meaning of the term *libel* is false news).

For more than a quarter of a century, the courts of this country have been struggling with the problems that defamation suits present. What, if any, kinds of mistakes should be allowed without liability? Should these standards of fault be changed according to the class of the person who claims to have been libeled? What kinds of damage awards are appropriate in what cases? What are the motives involved in bringing suits? Are some of these motives suspect? If so, how should the courts deal with these suits? Of course, the fundamental question is this: Should our society protect both freedom of expression and freedom from false attacks on personal reputation, and if so, how?

In the following pages real rather than hypothetical libel suits will be examined. These cases illustrate how the law and the courts have sought to resolve the fundamental conflict of free expression and secure reputation. In the process of attempting to strike a proper balance between these sometimes conflicting claims, the courts have dealt with all the other questions listed above and many more as well. The intent of these examples is not to offer a comprehensive review of libel law — there are many texts that serve such a purpose. Rather the purpose here is to provide some breadth and depth of understanding the problems of libel in a society that values freedom of expression. Perhaps the next time you see a news story that some celebrity is suing a gossip magazine for libel, you will recognize the real issues involved in the case and be able to make a more informed judgment about the merits of the competing claims of the parties involved.

2

Commissioner Sullivan and
The New York Times

The decade following the Supreme Court of
the United States' decision in 1954 that school segregation was unconstitutional was one of extreme
racial tension in the states of the old Confederacy.
Black insistence that their constitutional rights be
recognized and guaranteed was usually met with
white intransigence. Under the leadership of such
men as Martin Luther King, Jr., the black communities brought their grievances to the attention of
the American public through demonstrations and
reinforced those demonstrations through court
actions. The white communities of the South at
times responded with violence as well as their own
legal actions, bringing to bear whatever sanctions
of the criminal law they found available.

In few Southern communities was this conflict more evident than in Montgomery, Alabama.
The first direct-action black challenge to racial seg-

regation began in Montgomery on 1 December 1955 when Mrs. Rosa Parks, a seamstress, refused to give her bus seat to a white man and was arrested for violating state segregation laws. This act led to a bus boycott by black riders and the organization of the Montgomery Improvement Association led by Dr. King. King was arrested and convicted of violating an Alabama antiboycotting law. His house was bombed, and his life was threatened in midnight phone calls. The Montgomery Improvement Association first sought to end bus segregation through negotiations with the city, and when these efforts failed, they brought suit in federal court, which led to a November 1956 decision by the Supreme Court of the United States that the Alabama bus segregation laws were unconstitutional. The buses were desegregated, but white bitterness remained.

The financial demands of both the affirmative legal actions and the defense against criminal prosecutions were a major burden for the civil rights movement. The costs of litigation were substantial, involving not only court trials, lawyers fees, and fines but also often included the added financial burden of lengthy appeals processes in both state and federal courts. One means used to

meet these demands was active solicitation of con-
tributions in Northern communities. An example
of such solicitation was the full page ad placed in
The New York Times on 29 March 1960 by a group
called the Committee to Defend Martin Luther
King and the Struggle for Freedom in the South.
The text of the ad said in part:

> In Montgomery, Alabama, after students
> sang "My Country, 'Tis of Thee" on the State
> Capitol steps, their leaders were expelled
> from school, and truckloads of police armed
> with shotguns and tear-gas ringed the Ala-
> bama State College Campus. When the en-
> tire student body protested to state authori-
> ties by refusing to reregister, their dining
> hall was padlocked in an attempt to starve
> them into submission. . . .
>
> Again and again the Southern violators
> have answered Dr. King's peaceful protests
> with intimidation and violence. They have
> bombed his home almost killing his wife and
> child. They have assaulted his person. They
> have arrested him seven times—for "speed-
> ing," "loitering" and similar "offenses." And
> now they have charged him with "perj-
> ury"—a *felony* under which they could im-
> prison him for *ten years*. Obviously, their real

purpose is to remove him physically as the leader to whom the students and millions of others—look for guidance and support, and thereby to intimidate *all* leaders who may rise in the South. . . .

We must extend ourselves above and beyond moral support and render the material help so urgently needed by those who are taking the risks, facing jail, and even death in a glorious re-affirmation of our Constitution and its Bill of Rights.

We urge you to join hands with our fellow Americans in the South by supporting, with your dollars, this Combined Appeal for all three needs—the defense of Martin Luther King—the support of the embattled students—and the struggle for the right-to-vote.

The ad was signed by sixty-four well-known Americans, both black and white, representing primarily the fields of entertainment, labor, and letters. Among the signers were Harry Belafonte, Marlon Brando, Nat King Cole, Dorothy Dandridge, Sammy Davis, Jr., Nat Hentoff, Mahalia Jackson, John Lewis, Viveca Lindfors, Sidney Poitier, A. Philip Randolph, Elmer Rice, Jackie Robinson, Eleanor Roosevelt, Maureen Stapleton,

12

Norman Thomas, Kenneth Tynan, and Shelley Winters.

While the ad succeeded in raising legal defense funds in the North, it also succeeded in raising ire in the South. Urged on by the rabid editorializing of the *Montgomery Advertiser,* officials of the City of Montgomery complained, charging that the ad contained false statements that were injurious. The *Times* rejected their demand for a printed retraction, and on 19 April Montgomery Mayor Earl James and City Commissioners Frank Parks and L. B. Sullivan each filed a $500,000 damage suit against *The New York Times*. Also named in the complaint were four Alabama clergymen whose names had appeared as signers of the ad. Eight days later Alabama Governor John Patterson announced his intention to file his own suit against the paper for the same ad. In a letter to the *Times* Governor Patterson demanded a printed retraction of two paragraphs in the ad that he charged were false and defamatory. These passages dealt with the incident at Alabama State College and the arrest record of Dr. King. Regarding the first passage, the facts were that while police were deployed near the college campus, they did not "ring" it as charged. Most students, but not "the entire student body," protested, and the dining hall was never actually padlocked. Regarding the second passage, Dr. King had been arrested four rather than seven times.

In response to the Governor's complaint, the *Times* printed the following retraction on 16 May:

> The advertisement containing the statements to which Governor Patterson objects was received by The Times in the regular course of business from and paid for by a recognized advertising agency in behalf of a group which included among its subscribers well-known citizens.
>
> The publication of an advertisement does not constitute a factual news report by The Times nor does it reflect the judgment or the opinion of the editors of The Times. Since publication of the advertisement, The Times made an investigation and consistent with its policy of retracting and correcting any errors or misstatements which may appear in its columns, herewith retracts the two paragraphs complained of by the Governor.
>
> The New York Times never intended to suggest by the publication of the advertisement that the Honorable John Patterson, either in his capacity as Governor or as ex-

officio chairman of the Board of Education of
the State of Alabama, or otherwise, was
guilty of "grave misconduct or improper actions and omissions." To the extent that anyone can fairly conclude from the statement
that any such charge was made, The New
York Times hereby apologizes to the Honor-
able John Patterson therefor.

No retraction was published for the Montgomery
city officials, none of whom were mentioned in the
ad, because The *Times* refused to acknowledge that
there was any possibility of offense to these persons. Even the retraction that was published
achieved nothing. On 30 May an unsatisfied Governor Patterson filed suit against *The New York
Times* asking for $1 million in damages. When this
claim was added to the three existing ones, the paper and the selected black clergymen found that
they were being asked to pay a total of $2.5 million
in compensation for the errors that appeared in
the 29 March advertisement. *The New York Times*
was threatened even more by the filing of a series
of large libel suits by other Southern officials in reaction to a series of articles on conditions in the
South by Harrison Salisbury, one of the *Times'*
most respected reporters. The obvious purpose of

all this legal action against the *Times* was to discourage the paper's extensive reporting about Southern attempts to maintain racial segregation.

The first legal problem to be settled was a rather technical one with major significance for both sides. The question was whether *The New York Times* was a corporation doing business in Alabama and thus, for legal purposes, a citizen of Alabama. The United States Constitution states that suits between citizens of different states are to be tried in federal court. Thus, if the paper were not a citizen of Alabama, the suit against it would have to be tried in federal court, and it was on this basis that the *Times* moved to have the state court suits against it dismissed. In late July 1960 the case arising from the attempt to dismiss the libel suits was heard in a local Alabama court. Evidence was presented to show that *The New York Times* had hired an Alabama reporter on a part-time basis and that this reporter had written stories in Alabama that were phoned to the *Times* in New York City. It was argued that this arrangement constituted doing business in Alabama, and the court agreed. This decision was promptly upheld by the Alabama Circuit Court of Appeals. Thus, even though *The New York Times* was a New York corporation, it was forced to defend itself against the libel suits in the state courts of Alabama. The history of civil rights litigation had shown that the state courts, presided over by elected judges, were more hostile toward blacks and their supporters than were the federal courts.

The first suit to come to trial was that filed by Montgomery Public Safety Commissioner L. B. Sullivan, seeking $500,000 in damages. A jury of twelve white men was chosen, and the trial began 1 November 1960. Attorneys for Commissioner Sullivan sought to show that he had been damaged by the ad, while *The New York Times* claimed that there was no intention to direct comments at Commissioner Sullivan and that he could not be even remotely associated with the statements in the ad. In other words, the *Times* argued that there was no identification as is required in a libel suit. Commissioner Sullivan's lawyers stated that they were also asking for punitive damages to punish the paper for its misconduct and to deter it and others from ever doing the like again.

Five witnesses were presented for Sullivan, all of whom testified that since he was commissioner of public safety and the ad dealt with the conduct of law enforcement, they connected the ad with him. On cross examination all five testified that they did not believe the statements in the ad and that their opinion of Commissioner Sullivan had not been affected. Furthermore, three of the witnesses stated that they had not seen the ad until it was shown to them by Sullivan's lawyers. The final witness on behalf of Sullivan was the commissioner himself. Direct testimony and cross examination established that while parts of the ad could not have applied to him and no one had acted unfavorably toward him as a result of the ad, Commissioner Sullivan still felt that the general tone of the ad was libelous and that his character had been besmirched. In sum, an outside observer might fairly conclude that the evidence presented on behalf of Commissioner Sullivan failed to establish that there had been any damage from the ad.

Lawyers for *The New York Times* began their defense by arguing that the judge should dismiss the suit because no case had been established for Commissioner Sullivan's complaint. Alabama State Circuit Court Judge Walter Jones refused this request. Witnesses for the *Times* testified to two points. First, there could have been no malice in the publication of the ad since it had been accepted in the regular course of business. Furthermore, the *Times* had depended upon the prestige of the sixty-four celebrity signers of the ad as a guarantee of its accuracy. Second, the ad neither directly nor indirectly referred to Commissioner Sullivan. However, the jury took only two hours and twenty minutes to reach a verdict in favor of Commissioner Sullivan and to award him the full $500,000 damages he sought.

An understanding of this verdict can be realized by examining the Alabama libel law under which Sullivan brought his suit and the way Judge Jones instructed the jury regarding the application of the law to the specific case. The law stated that a libelous statement tended to injure a person's reputation or expose that person to public contempt. A jury should first have found that a statement was injurious. Second, it had to establish that the statement was made about the plaintiff. In Sullivan's case Judge Jones explained that suggestion of misconduct by the public agency headed by Sullivan would constitute a statement about Sullivan. Third, the jury needed to determine whether the statement was true. The defendant, *The New York Times,* was required to show that the statement was true in all particulars. If the *Times* could prove that everything published was true, there would be no case. If the statement was in any way false, the jury was invited to presume injury even if there had been no trial evidence showing injury. In other words, Judge Jones instructed the jury to use the strict liability standard to decide whether the newspaper was at fault. Fourth, the jury needed to find actual malice if punitive damages were to be awarded. While the instructions to the jury provided no clear definition of the term *malice,* the judge did explain that malice must be assumed unless a full retraction had been published. Malice would not be disproven by a showing of good motives and/or belief in the truth of the published statement. Motivation and belief in truth were relevant only to determine the amount of punitive damages the jury might decide to award. Within this legal framework the finding against the *Times* and its four codefendants was hardly surprising. The jury did not indicate what portion of the award was for *general* damages, that is, for actual injury, and what portion was for punitive damage.

For a number of reasons *The New York Times* rejected this verdict. It viewed the finding of libel as unjust and the damage award as excessive. In addition this case would establish an uncomfortable precedent for the other libel suits that were still to be tried. And so the long process of appeal was begun.

Until the appeal of the Sullivan case had been decided, the *Times* asked that the trials of the other suits be delayed. The continued cooperation of the Alabama judiciary in the punitive intent of all this legal action was demonstrated when this commonsense motion was denied. The trial of a second suit, that of Montgomery Mayor Earl James, began at the end of January 1961. The testimony presented at this trial essentially duplicated that presented in the first trial. Like Commissioner Sullivan, Mayor James stated that his reputation had been severely damaged but admitted during cross examination that he still enjoyed a good reputation in the community in spite of the ad. As in the first case, the all-white jury found no difficulty in rendering a verdict for the plaintiff and awarding him the full $500,000 damages asked.

Meanwhile, in addition to denying motions for continuance and motions for a new trial on the basis of judicial error, the Alabama courts also ruled that the four black clergymen who were the

Times' fellow defendants in the libel suits had forfeited their right of appeal. The four had been found guilty in both trials even though the evidence presented in both cases was that their names had been appended to the ad without either their knowledge or permission. The punitive and vindictive motives for the libel suits were confirmed by efforts to freeze the black clergymen's bank accounts and other assets and to take possession of their cars and other personal property to satisfy the judgment for Commissioner Sullivan. These efforts began even before the second libel suit had come to trial.

The appeal of *New York Times V. Sullivan* finally did reach the Alabama Supreme Court. Central to that appeal was the point that the paper was not a resident of the state and could not properly be sued in state court. On 30 August 1962, almost two years after the original trial, the Alabama Supreme Court handed down a fifty-nine page decision rejecting the *Times'* appeal. The court took the position that there was no difference between distributing libel within the state and printing and publishing it there, reaffirming the view that a publication could be sued in any locality where the publication was distributed. In addition the

22

court refused to find the size of the libel award excessive because the *Times* had shown "irresponsibility" in printing the ad when prior news stories in the *Times* "demonstrated the falsity of the allegations in the advertisement" and had also refused to print a retraction.

Having exhausted the possibilities of appeal in the courts of the state of Alabama, the *Times* appealed to the Supreme Court of the United States. The Supreme Court agreed to consider the case, heard the arguments, and finally handed down a verdict in 1964 unanimously reversing the original conviction. For six of the Justices, Associate Justice William Brennan wrote a landmark decision in the area of private libel. While many technical and procedural grounds for a reversal existed, such as the absence of identification of Sullivan in the ad, Justice Brennan broke new ground by examining directly the substantive issues of the case in the context of the freedom of speech guarantee of the First Amendment:

> We are required in this case to determine for the first time the extent to which the constitutional protection for speech and press limit a State's power to award damages in a libel

action brought by a public official against
critics of his official conduct.

The decision began with a review of the Alabama
libel law, noting the authoritative position taken by
the Alabama courts on the issues of identification,
injury, and the strict liability standard for fault. It
then presented the central issue of the case as fol-
lows:

> The question before us is whether this rule
> of liability, as applied to an action brought
> by a public official against critics of his offi-
> cial conduct, abridges the freedom of speech
> and of the press that is guaranteed by the
> First and Fourteenth Amendments.

Because the First Amendment deals only with the
federal government, the Fourteenth Amendment
was noted as the long established legal basis for
applying the freedom of speech guarantee to state
laws. The decision continued:

> Thus we consider this case against the back-
> ground of a profound national commitment
> to the principle that debate on public issues
> should be uninhibited, robust, and wide-

open, and that it may well include vehement, caustic, and sometimes unpleasantly sharp attacks on government and public officials. . . . The present advertisement, as an expression of grievance and protest on one of the major public issues of our time, would seem clearly to qualify for the constitutional protection. The question is whether it forfeits that protection by the falsity of some of its factual statements and by its alleged defamation of respondent.

Authoritative interpretations of the First Amendment guarantees have consistently refused to recognize an exception for any test of truth—whether administered by judges, juries, or administrative officials—and especially one that puts the burden of proving truth on the speaker. . . . The constitutional protection does not turn upon "the truth, popularity, or social utility of the ideas and beliefs which are offered." . . . As Madison said, "Some degree of abuse is inseparable from the proper use of everything; and in no instance is this more true than in that of the press."

. . . Just as factual error affords no warrant for repressing speech that would otherwise be free, the same is true of injury to official reputation. Where judicial officers are involved, this Court has held that concern for the dignity and reputation of the courts does not justify the punishment as criminal contempt of criticism of the judge or his decision. . . . This is true even though the utterance contains "half-truths" and "misinformation." . . . Such repression can be justified, if at all, only by a clear and present danger of the obstruction of justice. . . . If judges are to be treated as "men of fortitude, able to thrive in a hardy climate," . . . surely the same must be true of other government officials, such as elected city commissioners. Criticism of their official conduct does not lose its constitutional protection merely because it is effective criticism and hence diminishes their official reputations.

. . . A rule compelling the critic of official conduct to guarantee the truth of all his factual assertions—and to do so on pain of libel judgments virtually unlimited in amount—leads to a comparable "self-censorship." Allowance of the defense of truth, with the burden of proving it on the defendant, does not mean that only false speech will be deterred. Even courts accepting this defense as an adequate safeguard have recognized the difficulties of adducing legal proofs that the alleged libel was true in all its factual particulars. . . . Under such a rule, would-be critics of official conduct may be

deterred from voicing their criticism, even
though it is believed to be true and even
though it is in fact true, because of doubt
whether it can be proved in court or fear of
the expense of having to do so. They tend to
make only statements which "steer far wider
of the unlawful zone." . . . The rule thus
dampens the vigor and limits the variety of
public debate. It is inconsistent with the First
and Fourteenth Amendments.

Having thus forcefully rejected the strict liability standard of fault as it had been set forth by
the Alabama law and courts, Brennan stated what
the standard of fault for a libel action by a public
official should be.

The constitutional guarantees require,
we think, a federal rule that prohibits a public official from recovering damages for a defamatory falsehood relating to his official
conduct unless he proves that the statement
was made with "actual malice" —that is, with
knowledge that it was false or with reckless
disregard of whether it was false or not.

While there were many grounds that might
have been used for setting aside the outrageous at-

tack on press freedom by the Alabama officials and courts (such as identification or even the jurisdiction of the state court in this case), the approach taken by Justice Brennan and the five other Justices who joined in his opinion was to focus on the question of fault. This approach established a principle that would apply to other cases including the three other suits that had been filed against *The New York Times* over the disputed ad. Brennan observed that public officials have access to the news media and are thus able to correct most errors by getting the truth, as they see it, published.

Finally, Brennan's lead opinion indicated recognition of the punitive motives of the Alabama officials but stated explicitly that there was insufficient evidence to sustain a judgment for the officials using this new "knowing falsehood or reckless disregard for truth" standard.

> Applying these standards, we conclude that the proof presented to show actual malice lacks the convincing clarity which the constitutional standard demands, and hence that it would not constitutionally sustain the judgment for respondent [Sullivan] under the proper rule of law.

The three other Justices agreed that Sullivan should lose but offered different views of what the law should be. These three were Justices Black, Douglas, and Goldberg. All three would go beyond the knowing falsehood or reckless disregard (actual malice) standard. Justices Black and Douglas said,

> We would, I think, more faithfully interpret the First Amendment by holding that at the very least it leaves the people and the press free to criticize officials and discuss public affairs with impunity.

Justices Goldberg and Douglas put it this way:

> In my view, the First and Fourteenth Amendments to the Constitution afford to the citizens and the press an absolute, unconditional privilege to criticize official conduct despite the harm which may flow from excesses and abuses.

In other words all three said that the public should be able freely to criticize the official conduct of elected officials, even including the right to lie. Any libel action for comment on official conduct should be impossible. To support this position Black and Douglas pointed to the multiple libel suits filed by Alabama officials.

> In fact, briefs before us show that in Alabama there are now pending eleven libel suits by local and state officials against the *Times* seeking $5,600,000 and five such suits against the Columbia Broadcasting System seeking $1,700,000. Moreover, this technique for harassing and punishing a free press— now that it has been shown to be possible— is by no means limited to cases with racial overtones; it can be used in other fields where public feelings may make local as well as out-of-state newspapers easy prey for libel verdict seekers.

For Black and Douglas the lifting of all restrictions was essential to protect press freedom.

In his opinion Justice Goldberg, joined by Justice Douglas, did place a limit on press freedom from libel suits:

> This is not to say that the Constitution protects defamatory statements directed against the private conduct of a public official or private citizen. . . . Purely private def-

amation has little to do with the political
ends of a self-governing society. The imposi-
tion of liability for private defamation does
not abridge the freedom of public speech.

With this decision four years of litigation that
had certainly been costly for *The New York Times*
came to an end. Montgomery City Commissioners
Sullivan and Parks, Mayor James, and Governor
Patterson had been prohibited by the language of
the Supreme Court's opinions from taking legal action against criticism of their public policies that
might appear in *The New York Times* or anywhere
else. In addition, the Court had established a new
standard for judging fault for published errors. In
regard to the official conduct of elected officials,
this new standard required proof that the published statement was known to be false or published with reckless disregard for its truth or
falsity. Three members of the Court would, in fact,
protect any statement about the official conduct of
public officials.

While this "first time" consideration of the issue by the Supreme Court of the United States led
to a landmark decision that provided a standard
for fault that would seem to provide broad, new

protection for freedom of speech and press, a number of issues that were not before the Court remain to be considered. Does this new standard apply only to elected officials? What kinds of evidence can be used in a trial to prove knowing falsehood or reckless disregard? When fault is proven, what kinds of damage awards are appropriate? Is there a connection between fault and damages? And has the knowing falsehood-reckless disregard/actual malice standard really established protection for the press from meritless libel suits? The cases considered in subsequent chapters will present some answers for these questions.

3

Barry Goldwater and *fact* Magazine

The decision of the Supreme Court of the United States in *New York Times v. Sullivan* established a demanding standard for proving fault in libel cases involving public officials. In such cases the plaintiff must prove not only that the published material was false but also that it was published either with knowledge that the material was false or with reckless disregard for whether it was false or not. In trial the plaintiff must present evidence of such knowledge or recklessness with "convincing clarity" to the jury. A central question is how such evidence is to be secured. The jury is apparently being asked to evaluate the state of mind of the defendant as the process of publication was under way. The way in which such evidence can be developed is illustrated by the libel suit brought by Barry Goldwater, the widely known Republican senator from Arizona and Republican candidate for president of the United States in 1964, against publisher Ralph Ginzburg and his magazine *fact*. This suit was the first major libel case involving a public official tried under the *Times v. Sullivan* rule.

The 1964 presidential campaign between Barry Goldwater and Lyndon B. Johnson was clearly characterized by uninhibited, robust, and wide-open public debate even if much of that debate had little to do with the major campaign issues. This campaign was one of the dirtiest and most vicious of this century. The lack of uncertainty about the outcome of the election seemed only to stimulate the candidates' partisans to greater malice. A battle of paperback books included such items as Fred J. Cook's *Barry Goldwater Extremist of the Right,* which sought to establish Goldwater's ties to various organizations of the radical right, and John A. Stormer's *None Dare Call It Treason,* which through spurious quotation and documentation attempted to establish the Communist domination of all liberal politicians and political ideas. Even the two major political parties got into the act. Republican party offices around the country distributed copies of *A Choice Not an Echo* by Phyllis Schafly even though it was in large part an attack on the liberal wing of the Republican party. Among Democrats a popular item was *The Goldwa-*

ter Cartoon Book edited by Pat Frank containing a selection of irresponsible political cartoons attacking Goldwater.

The *piece de resistance* of this unsavory campaign was the September-October 1964 issue of *fact* magazine. On magazine stands throughout the country the front cover of *fact* proclaimed in letters more than an inch high, "1,189 Psychiatrists Say Goldwater Is Psychologically Unfit To Be President!" Under the heading, "What Psychiatrists Say About Goldwater," the back cover of the magazine provided the browser with choice extracts from the material inside.

> B.G. is in my opinion emotionally unstable, immature, volatile, unpredictable, hostile, and mentally unbalanced. He is totally unfit for public office and a menace to society.

> My clinical impression is that he is a paranoid personality with dominance of subjective views over objective.

> His theme is "freedom"—but from what? Unconsciously, it seems to be from his mother's domination.

> B.G.'s proneness to aggressive behavior and destructiveness indicates an attempt to prove his manliness.

> He consciously wants to destroy the world with atomic bombs. He is a mass-murderer at heart and a suicide. He is amoral and immoral. A dangerous lunatic!

> As a human being he is to be pitied. As President of the United States he would be a disaster.

Those who paid $1.25 to take a copy of *fact* home discovered that this sixty-four page issue, subtitled "The Unconscious of a Conservative: A Special Issue on the Mind of Barry Goldwater," was in two parts. The first section was a highly selective biography of Goldwater written by *fact* publisher Ralph Ginzburg. The biography was in large part a cut-and-paste job based on a number of other magazine articles about the senator, campaign biographies, and *Why Not Victory?* and other writings by the senator. From these sources, each one clearly credited, Ginzburg put together a word portrait of a psychological misfit, the product of an emotionally disturbed home, and the victim of at least two nervous breakdowns. Ginzburg's own characterization of Goldwater referred to "his paralyzing, deep-seated, irrational fear," and "his paranoid divorce from reality."

The major portion of the magazine was devoted to a selection of comments received from psychiatrists polled by *fact*. This selection was preceded by the following three-paragraph explanation:

On July 24, one week after Barry Goldwater received the Republican nomination, FACT sent a questionnaire to all of the nation's 12,356 psychiatrists asking, "Do you believe Barry Goldwater is psychologically fit to serve as President of the United States?" (The names were supplied by the American Medical Association.)

In all, 2,417 psychiatrists responded. Of these, 571 said they did not know enough about Goldwater to answer the question; 657 said they thought Goldwater was psychologically fit; and 1,189 said that he was not. (It might be pointed out that the majority of those who thought Goldwater was psychologically fit nevertheless said they were not voting for him.)

FACT'S questionnaire left room for "Comments" and over a quarter of a million

words of professional opinion were received.
On the next 41 pages we present a sampling
of these comments, which, all together, constitute the most intensive character analysis
ever made of a living human being.

The selection contained quotations from 162 questionnaires, 61 of which were signed either "Anonymous" or "name withheld." Some of the signed
comments were critical of *fact*.

What type of yellow rag are you oper-
ating? I have never in my life witnessed such
a shabby attempt to smear a political candidate. I would suggest that you change the
name of your magazine to "Fancy", or better,
"Smear"!
—Marvin J. Allison, M.D.
Richmond, Va.

If you will send me written authoriza-
tion from Senator Goldwater and arrange for
an appointment, I shall be happy to send
you a report concerning his mental state.
The same goes for you.
—Hubert Miller, M.D.
Detroit

> Your "survey" raises doubts in my
> mind as to your psychological fitness to pub-
> lish any national magazine, especially one
> named "FACT."
>> —Edmund V. Cowdry, Jr., M.D.
>> St. Louis

However, the overwhelming majority of the quotations were in the tone of those presented on the
back cover of the magazine.

There was a good bit of unfavorable reaction
to the publication of this issue of *fact* and the
large-scale advertising promotion of the issue
which included a full page ad in *The New York
Times*. Perhaps the sharpest response was that of
the American Medical Association. In a press release the AMA questioned the whole sampling
procedure and vehemently denied having supplied
fact with a list of psychiatrists. The names had actually come from a mailing list rented from a company licensed by the AMA to supply such
information.

The most significant reaction to this fifth issue of *fact* came from Senator Goldwater. On 2
September 1965, almost exactly a year after the
first ads for this issue appeared, Goldwater filed a
$2 million libel suit in the Federal District Court in

New York City against *fact,* publisher Ralph Ginzburg, and managing editor Warren Boroson. The
Supreme Court's decision in the Sullivan case the
year before was obviously taken into consideration
in preparing the suit, *Goldwater v. Ginzburg,* which
claimed that the publication had shown actual
malice. Ginzburg responded in a press release two
days later claiming that this magazine had per-
formed a valuable service in presenting the information about Goldwater. He viewed the dispute
between *fact* and Goldwater in terms of a conflict
between freedom of speech and repression, and he
felt that freedom would win.

The thirty-two months between filing the
suit and the actual trial were taken up with more
than just waiting for the case to come up in an
overcrowded court schedule. Much of this time
was used for the process of pretrial discovery in
which both sides sought to establish evidence
needed to support their positions. During this
process Senator Goldwater's lawyers needed to develop the facts to prove with convincing clarity
that Ginzburg and Boroson published what they
knew to be false or demonstrated reckless disregard for whether the material was false or not.
During this same period the lawyers for *fact*

sought information to prove the truth of what had been published.

In a 1967 opinion in *St. Amant v. Thompson*, Justice Byron White, writing for the majority of the Supreme Court of the United States, had explained what evidence was needed to prove reckless or knowing falsehood:

> There must be sufficient evidence to permit the conclusion that the defendant in fact entertained serious doubts as to the truth of his publication. Publishing with such doubts shows reckless disregard for truth or falsity and demonstrates actual malice. . . .
>
> The defendant in a defamation action brought by a public official cannot, however, automatically insure a favorable verdict by testifying that he published with a belief that the statements were true. The finder of fact [the jury] must determine whether the publication was indeed made in good faith. Professions of good faith will be unlikely to prove persuasive, for example, where a story is fabricated by the defendant, is the product of his imagination, or is based wholly on an unverified anonymous telephone call. Nor will they be likely to prevail when the publisher's allegations are so inherently improb-

able that only a reckless man would have put them in circulation. Likewise, recklessness may be found where there are obvious reasons to doubt the veracity of the informant or the accuracy of his reports.

The evidence developed in discovery involved both documents and testimony. Each side requested that the other side submit documents that would bear on the case. Goldwater's attorneys asked for notes and memoranda exchanged by Ginzburg and Boroson. They asked for the magazine articles and books from which the quotations used in Ginzburg's article had been drawn. They also asked for the original returned questionnaires that provided the material in the second part of the September-October 1964 issue of *fact*. Ginzburg's lawyers refused to submit some of this material, in particular the original questionnaires, on the grounds that the editorial process that went into producing this issue of *fact* was confidential and not subject to inspection. However, Goldwater's lawyers then asked for and received a court order directing Ginzburg to provide the requested material. Ginzburg's lawyers requested Goldwater's medical and military service records.

Using the documents as a basis for questions, testimony under oath (called depositions) was taken from the parties involved in the suit. Senator Goldwater and his wife were questioned in detail about elements in the medical records that might point to a psychological disorder. Ginzburg was questioned about the development of the Goldwater issue of *fact* and in particular about his decisions to include, exclude, or alter quotations that appeared in the magazine. He was also pressed to identify unnamed sources who had been cited in his biography of Goldwater.

The trial, which began Monday, 6 May 1968, took three weeks to complete. At the outset the opposing lawyers presented the positions of the two sides. For Goldwater, attorney Roger Robb claimed that *fact* had "published false, scandalous, defamatory statements knowing them to be false or recklessly not caring if they were true or not." Proof of this claim would be needed to establish actual malice and win the suit. Ginzburg's lawyer, Harris Steinburg, presented a two-part defense of his client. First, even though the magazine was "racy and tough," the article was good journalism and entirely true. Second, even if the material were not entirely true, "the defendants published

43

the articles in good faith, with no intention to lie, and in the belief that they were making a rightful, responsible contribution to predicting how a candidate might perform if elected."

With the issues now clearly drawn, the case for Goldwater began with an immediate attempt to prove that statements in *fact* were false. The Senator's wife was presented as a witness, and she testified that her husband had never had a nervous breakdown and had never professionally visited a psychiatrist. The following morning Goldwater himself took the witness stand to begin what was to be six full days of testimony and cross-examination. In direct testimony he restated the previously established points that he had never seen a psychiatrist or had a nervous breakdown. When asked about the specific incident that had been characterized by *fact* as a mental breakdown, the Senator said that once when he was thoroughly exhausted he had taken a ten-day vacation with his family. Personal medical records and his military fitness record were introduced as supporting evidence. The final point established in Goldwater's two days of direct testimony was that the senator had suffered mentally from *fact*'s "totally dishonest" picture of him. This testimony was presented to establish that Goldwater had been damaged by *fact*'s false characterizations of him.

Following his direct testimony Senator Goldwater was subjected to almost four full days of cross-examination by Attorney Steinburg. The basic thrust of the questioning was an effort to show that while *fact*'s statements might have been false in some details, the general picture of Goldwater was accurate. His private life, his military career, and his record as United States senator were probed in an effort to show qualities that might support the broad diagnosis of paranoia. When this effort failed, Steinburg tried to reverse roles to make *fact* appear to be the victim rather than Goldwater. An example of this approach was the questioning of Goldwater's motives for bringing suit. He was charged with seeking publicity for his senatorial campaign, and he denied the charge. He was accused of picking on *fact* rather than strong opponents such as the Columbia Broadcasting System or *The New York Times*. Goldwater answered that their attacks on him lacked the malice of *fact*'s attack. He indicated that the basic reasons for his suit were the four charges that he was an "anal character," a latent homosexual, paranoid, and similar to Adolf Hitler.

After Senator Goldwater completed his testimony and cross-examination, additional evidence was presented on his behalf dealing with the question of malice. In order to prove a reckless disregard for truth, testimony was presented by professional pollster B. W. Roper regarding the *fact* survey about Goldwater. Roper testified that the number of responses was too small to be statistically valid, that the questions were slanted against Goldwater, that no questions were asked regarding Goldwater's election opponent Lyndon Johnson, and that it was unclear whether *fact* was asking for a personal or a professional response.

The last two days of the case for the plaintiff involved the presentation of materials developed during the all-important discovery process. Senator Goldwater's lawyer read into the record and for the jury documents and depositions that had been given. While such recitations can be boring for the jury, the material was essential in the process of proving knowing or reckless falsehood. A letter was read showing that, before he had begun any research, Ginzburg had determined to present Goldwater as a paranoid personality. In the Goldwater biography the jury was repeatedly shown examples in which a single sentence or phrase with an unfavorable connotation was drawn from what, in its totality, was clearly a favorable comment. While the Goldwater biography made reference to "people around Goldwater" or "European reporters," in his deposition Ginzburg was unable to identify these people or anyone else who might have supplied the information in question. But clearly the most damaging evidence was the contrast between materials in the questionnaires that had been returned to *fact* and the quotations that appeared in the magazine. There were numerous phrases taken out of context, separate responses combined to appear as one, anonymous statements appearing to have identifiable sources, and even statements changed by Ginzburg to enhance or produce negative effects.

The defendants' case was developed on two levels. First, it was argued that the controversial issue of *fact* was fundamentally accurate, truth being a whole defense in libel cases. If inaccuracies appeared, they arose from the sources used rather than any errors or omissions by Boroson and Ginzburg. In this regard pretrial depositions from five of the psychiatrists who had participated in the survey were read. Each said that his published opinion was an accurate representation of his personal (not professional) evaluation. In addition, Warren Boroson testified that the publication arose out of an honest effort to assess Senator Goldwater's fitness to be president. He denied writing anything false about Goldwater and denied any malicious intent on the part of anyone at *fact*. This concluding statement was *fact*'s second line of defense: even if some of the statements made were false, they were not knowing or reckless falsehoods.

The major portion of the case for *fact* magazine rested on the testimony of its publisher, Ralph Ginzburg. In direct testimony Ginzburg represented himself as a conscientious journalist trying, to the best of his ability, to do his job. He characterized the issue of *fact* in question as a valuable historical contribution, claimed that he simply tried to make an accurate presentation of what people were saying about Goldwater, and stated unequivocally that he bore the senator no malice. To this extent Ginzburg's testimony forcefully paralleled Boroson's. Senator Goldwater's attorney, Roger Robb, used his cross-examination of Ginzburg to introduce many specific examples of published statements that had been drawn out of context or had in other ways deliberately misrepresented the original sources. Ginzburg was challenged to explain his editing and the alterations that the discovery process had revealed. On the basis of this cross-examination Ginzburg was charged with publishing statements he knew to be false with a reckless disregard for their truth. If the jury was to accept these charges, the actual malice needed to award damages would be proven. Under this attack Ginzburg was forced to admit that statements in *fact* were false. However, he claimed that they were a fair and proper journalistic comment on a public figure.

On Friday, 24 May at the end of the third week of the trial, Judge Harold Tyler instructed the jury regarding the points of law in the case. He explained to the jurors that since Senator Goldwater was a public figure, they had to find that there had been malice in the publication to render a verdict against *fact*. A finding of malice depended on whether the jury believed that the defendant knew the material being published was untrue or that Ginzburg had shown a reckless disregard for its truth or falsity. The argument that the defendant was only publishing untrue statements that originated elsewhere would not be adequate justification for publishing such material.

Finally, if the jury found that Senator Goldwater had been libeled, it could award compensatory damages for actual injury, punitive damages to punish the defendant for his misdeed, or both.

While the trial had been lengthy, the jury's deliberations were brief. The verdict was returned the same afternoon that the jury received the case. Ralph Ginzburg and *fact* were found guilty of libel. Senator Goldwater was awarded $1 in *compensatory* damages, $25,000 in punitive damages from Ginzburg, and $50,000 in punitive damages from *fact*. Both the verdict and the nature of the damage award were a blow to Ginzburg because the award indicated that even though libel had been committed he and *fact* lacked the stature to inflict any real damage. Ginzburg, however, in a press release, indicated his intention to appeal and still presented the case as one involving freedom of speech:

> Some very important First Amendment rights are involved here. The price that I'm paying is $75,000 but the price that the American public will have to pay is incalculable. . . . Some of the stuff was not true, but it constituted fair opinion.

The United States Court of Appeals for the Second Circuit took slightly more than a year to hear the case and hand down a decision upholding the verdict against Ginzburg. It reviewed the trial record and found clear proof of the publication of knowing or reckless falsehoods. In his appeal Ginzburg had, among other points, emphasized the argument that he was merely reprinting what others had said about Goldwater. As with all the other issues, the court forcefully rejected this argument.

> Repetition of another's words does not release one of responsibility if the repeater knows that the words are false or inherently improbable, or there are obvious reasons to doubt the veracity of the author of the report. . . . Furthermore, in our case, Ginzburg added certain innuendos to some quoted statements and quoted other statements out of context in order to support his predetermined result.

This adverse decision by the court of appeals was appealed to the Supreme Court of the United States, and that court exercised its right to refuse to consider the case. While reasons for refusing to hear a case are not usually given, the Court majority may well have felt that the requirements for proof of reckless or knowing falsehood that had been enunciated in *St. Amant* had been met. The only written opinion was a dissent from this judgment written by Justice Hugo Black, joined by Justice William O. Douglas, who believed that the Court should have heard the case. Justice Black's consistent position was that the guarantee of freedom of speech is absolute and that any libel action violated that guarantee. He said,

> I cannot subscribe to the result the Court reaches today because I firmly believe that the First Amendment guarantees to each person in this country the unconditional right to print what he pleases about public affairs.

He restated his objection to the exception for actual malice in libel suits allowed in *New York Times v. Sullivan* and added:

> Extravagant, reckless statements and even claims which may not be true seem to me an inevitable and perhaps essential part of the process by which the voting public in-

forms itself of the qualities of a man who would be president. The decisions of the District Court and the Court of Appeals in this case can only have the effect of dampening political debate by making fearful and timid those who should under our Constitution feel totally free openly to criticize presidential candidates. Doubtless, the jury was justified in this case in finding that the Fact [*sic*] articles on Senator Goldwater were prepared with a reckless disregard of the truth, as many campaign articles unquestionably are. But, even if I believed in a balancing process to determine scope of the First Amendment, which I do not, the grave dangers of prohibiting or penalizing the publication of even the most inaccurate and misleading information seem to me to more than outweigh any gain, personal or social, that might result from permitting libel awards such as the one before the Court today. I firmly believe it is precisely because of these considerations that the First Amendment bars in absolute, unequivocal terms any abridgment by the Government of freedom of speech and press.

The decision by the Supreme Court of the United States not to hear an appeal ended the con-

troversy between *fact* and Senator Goldwater that
had begun with the publication of the Goldwater
issue of *fact* five years earlier. The senator's libel
suit was the first by a nationally prominent public
official using the knowing or reckless falsehood
standard for fault established in *New York Times v.
Sullivan*. The process of this litigation makes clear
how difficult it is to prove such fault. The plaintiff
must establish for the jury in a clear and convincing manner what was in the defendant's mind pri-
or to publication and the care, or lack thereof,
taken in making editorial judgments. Only
through detailed exploration can the plaintiff discover that the defendant knew what was being
published was false or that the defendant had
been recklessly indifferent in discovering whether
what was to be published was true or false. If a libel plaintiff is expected to prove this high degree
of fault, that plaintiff must be allowed to discover
if evidence of such fault exists.

The proper extent of pretrial discovery
(where there is a need to prove knowing or reckless falsehood) was finally determined eleven
years after the Goldwater-Ginzburg trial in the
1979 case of *Herbert v. Lando*. Colonel Anthony Herbert, a much decorated Korean War hero with

combat experience in the Vietnam conflict, charged that his superiors knew of and covered up atrocities committed by United States troops in Vietnam. Because the Vietnam conflict was becoming increasingly unpopular with the public in the early 1970s, Herbert naturally received much news media attention. His book about Vietnam, *Soldier,* became a best seller, and CBS news decided to do a profile on Herbert and his book for "60 Minutes." In the course of preparing the profile, program producer Barry Lando and reporter Mike Wallace began to have doubts about Herbert's story. Details did not check out. People had not been present at times and places that Herbert claimed. CBS discovered that the army had carefully investigated Herbert's charges and found them without substance. As the result of this investigation a very different profile was broadcast than the one originally planned. This February 1973 "60 Minutes" segment examined both the discrepancies in Herbert's story and the way in which the news media had so uncritically accepted and repeated Herbert's charges.

Herbert, who had cooperated with CBS and expected a complimentary profile, was angered by what had been broadcast and brought suit for libel against CBS, Wallace, and Lando. Because of modifications over the years to the *New York Times v. Sullivan* doctrine, Herbert was within that class of people required to prove knowing or reckless falsehood to win a libel suit. To this end his lawyers began a discovery process very much like that undertaken for Senator Goldwater. They demanded and received internal working memos regarding the program as well as all the film footage collected for the broadcast but not used. They also took lengthy depositions from those who worked on the broadcast including both Mike Wallace and Barry Lando.

During the questioning of Barry Lando, Herbert's lawyers sought to find out why certain decisions were made. Why was one person interviewed and another not? Why was one filmed response used and not another? The clear purpose of such questions was to discover if Lando used material that he knew was untrue or was recklessly unconcerned about the truth or falsity of the material. However, Lando refused to answer these questions claiming that such explorations into his state of mind and the editorial process used to prepare the broadcast were beyond the legitimate scope of the discovery process.

Herbert's lawyers brought the question of Lando's refusal to answer their questions before the judge in charge of this preliminary phase of their case. They argued that if Herbert was required to prove knowing or reckless falsehood, he must be allowed to ask and receive answers to the questions that might supply this proof. The judge agreed, and CBS appealed that ruling to the United States Court of Appeals for the Second Circuit arguing that this detailed exploration of the editorial process violated the freedom of the press guarantees of the First Amendment. When the court of appeals agreed with CBS, Herbert asked the Supreme Court of the United States to hear this case, which it did. The 1979 decision rendered in *Herbert v. Lando* supported Herbert's position. The Court's opinion called attention to the heavy burden involved in proving with convincing clarity that publication of knowing or reckless falsehoods had been made. Under those circumstances a libel plaintiff should be given the broadest latitude in seeking information to develop that proof. Lando and any future defendants in such libel suits would be required to answer questions about state of mind and editorial process.

The decision in *Herbert v. Lando* confirmed the propriety of the pretrial discovery process that had been used in the *Goldwater v. Ginzburg* suit. The Supreme Court of the United States recognized that if it was going to support the demanding, knowing or reckless falsehood standard of fault, a libel plaintiff must, in fairness, be allowed to ask for the information that might make it possible to prove such fault.

After the discovery process in Colonel Herbert's libel suit against CBS had dragged on for another six years, lawyers for CBS asked Charles S. Haight, Jr., the trial court judge overseeing the case, to grant CBS *summary judgment,* and he did so by dismissing nine of Herbert's eleven claims. The judge concluded that even after a total of almost twelve years of discovery Herbert had been unable to develop enough evidence to support most of his claims of broadcast falsehoods. Only two minor issues remained for a jury to consider. Both CBS and Herbert appealed this decision. Herbert asked that the entire case be reinstated while CBS asked for summary judgment on the last two items. On 15 January 1986 the Second Circuit Court of Appeals, the same court that had ruled against Herbert during the discovery process, granted the CBS request. No jury would ever hear Anthony Herbert's claim that CBS had broadcast reckless or knowing falsehoods about him. The appeals court concluded that even if there had been a couple of minor errors, the substance of the broadcast was true. However, it had cost CBS millions in legal fees before the courts were willing to recognize that Herbert's defamation suit was without merit.

The thirteen years of litigation in the Herbert suit against CBS is a landmark of sorts in the history of libel suits. On the one hand, it now appears that Herbert had very little grounds for his suit. This fact may have contributed to the excessive delay in bringing the case to trial. On the other hand, as the decision and opinion in *Herbert v. Lando* make clear, Herbert, as a public figure needing to prove reckless or knowing falsehood, had to be allowed the broadest latitude in the discovery process to develop the evidence needed to prove his case. In addition, the Herbert case illustrates that the present laws and legal processes involved in libel suits do not serve well the interests of either plaintiffs or defendants. There are many more illustrations of this point in subsequent chapters.

4

Police Defame George Rosenbloom

As *Goldwater v. Ginzburg* illustrates, the task of establishing fault for a public official in a libel case is demanding. Reckless disregard or knowing falsehood is much more difficult to prove than simple negligence. Thus, it is not surprising that in a series of cases that followed *New York Times v. Sullivan* the Supreme Court of the United States was encouraged to extend this higher standard of fault to people other than elected public officials. Beginning with *Rosenblatt v. Baer* in 1966 the Court responded favorably to these requests.

Frank Baer was the appointed director of the Belknap County, New Hampshire, recreation facility. A year after Baer had been discharged from his position Alfred Rosenblatt wrote in the *Laconia Evening Citizen* that the recreation area was now in much better financial shape. Baer sued, claiming that the article accused him of mismanagement, and was awarded $31,500. The Supreme Court of the United States reversed, holding that Baer should be considered a public official and must therefore prove reckless or knowing falsehood.

A year later the Court considered the cases of *Curtis Publishing Company v. Butts* and *Associated Press v. Walker*. In the first case, *The Saturday Evening Post* published an article suggesting that University of Georgia athletic director Wally Butts had conspired with University of Alabama football coach Bear Bryant to fix a football game between the two schools. A divided Supreme Court upheld the trial court award of $460,000 to Butts, concluding that while Butts was a public figure, he had successfully proven, in the words of Justice Hargan's opinion, that the *Post* had been guilty of "highly unreasonable conduct constituting an extreme departure from the standards of investigation and reporting ordinarily adhered to be responsible publishers."

In the companion case the Supreme Court set aside a jury award of $500,000 in compensatory damages to former Major General Edwin Walker. In a story filed by a college student working as an Associated Press stringer, Walker had been identified as a leader of the riots that accompanied the enrollment of the first black student at the University of Mississippi. Walker was present during the riots but denied acting as described in the article. The Court concluded that because of his notoriety Walker, like Butts, was a public figure. Since he had failed to prove reckless disregard or knowing falsehood in the Associated Press article, Walker's damage award was set aside.

The fourth case in this series was *Rosenbloom v. Metromedia*.

Many in law enforcement have long recognized the public relations benefits of campaigns to crack down on pornography. The general public responds favorably to a well-publicized war against smut. Further benefits are that such campaigns do not require extensive investigations and do not entail any real physical danger when making arrests. A minimum of effort can produce a maximum of favorable news coverage.

In the fall of 1963 the Special Investigations Squad of Philadelphia commanded by Captain Ferguson undertook a highly visible antipornography campaign. The investigation phase of the campaign involved Ferguson's visits to some twenty newsstands where he purchased a collection of magazines that he had flipped through and decided were obscene. In trial testimony Ferguson explained that "anytime the private parts is showing of the female or the private parts is shown of males [sic]" he would conclude that the publication was legally obscene. Such a definition was completely contrary to that enunciated by the Supreme Court of the United States in *Roth v. United States* in 1957 and amplified in subsequent decisions.

On the basis of Captain Ferguson's "extensive" investigation well-publicized arrests of newsstand operators and employees were undertaken. Also arrested was George Rosenbloom, a distributor of nudist magazines, who arrived to make a delivery at one location while the police raid was in progress. Following up on this hot new lead, police obtained a search warrant and raided Rosenbloom's house and warehouse three days later. Rosenbloom was arrested a second time. The warrant was sought by the police and issued by a magistrate even though the longstanding, clear, and unequivocal position of the Supreme Court of the United States was that nudist magazines are not obscene.

To make sure that all phases of his anti-smut campaign were adequately publicized, Captain Ferguson telephoned local news radio stations, one of the local newspapers, and a wire service to

tell them about his raid on this major distributor
of "obscene" material. On the basis of the information supplied by Ferguson, radio station WIP,
which broadcast news every half hour, presented
the following report on their 6:00 P.M. broadcast on
4 October 1963:

City Cracks Down on Smut Merchants

The Special Investigations Squad
raided the home of George Rosenbloom in
the 1800 block of Vesta Street this afternoon.
Police confiscated 1,000 allegedly obscene
books at Rosenbloom's home and arrested
him on charges of possession of obscene literature. The Special Investigations Squad
also raided a barn in the 20 Hundred block
of Welsh Road near Bustleton Avenue and
confiscated 3,000 obscene books. Captain
Ferguson says that he believes they have hit
the supply of a main distributor of obscene
material in Philadelphia.

This news report with minor changes (adding the
word "allegedly" in the third sentence) was broadcast
a total of seven times over the next twelve hours.

Following his arrests Rosenbloom consulted
his lawyer who confirmed that nudist magazines
were not legally obscene and that Captain Fer-

guson's standard for judgment was without basis
in law. A suit was brought on behalf of Rosenbloom in Federal District Court seeking an injunc-
tion to prohibit police interference with Rosenbloom's business. That suit resulted in news
reports including the following WIP broadcast at
6:30 A.M. on 21 October:

> Federal District Judge Lord will hear
> arguments today from two publishers and a
> distributor all seeking an injunction against
> Philadelphia Police Commissioner Howard
> Leary . . . District Attorney James C.
> Crumlish . . . a local television station and a
> newspaper . . . ordering them to lay off the
> smut literature racket.
>
> The girlie-book peddlers say the police
> crackdown and continued reference to their
> borderline literature as smut or filth is hurt-
> ing their business. Judge Lord refused to is-
> sue a temporary injunction when he was
> first approached. It will set a precedent . . .
> and if the injunction is not granted . . . it
> could signal an even more intense effort to
> rid the city of pornography.

This broadcast, which did not mention Rosenbloom by name, was presented with some varia-

tions a total of thirteen times over a period of twelve days. Those bringing the suit were Rosenbloom, his wife, and the publisher of the magazines that Rosenbloom distributed.

The next important legal action came seven months later in May 1964. A state court jury acquitted Rosenbloom of all the charges that had been brought against him by the Philadelphia police. The trial court judge correctly instructed the jury that as a matter of law nudist magazines are not obscene, a fact the Philadelphia police and prosecutors had ignored. This trial result confirmed that Captain Ferguson's report to WIP had been false and that WIP's subsequent broadcasts about the case had contained falsehoods.

On the basis of his experience with Philadelphia law enforcement authorities and news agencies, George Rosenbloom concluded that he had been defamed. He had been identified in published false and damaging reports. The source of his original troubles, and the damaging reports that flowed from them, was clearly Captain Ferguson. However, another principle, that of *sovereign immunity,* prevented a successful suit against Ferguson. Pennsylvania law bars defamation suits for statements by government officials.

The extensiveness of this protection is illustrated in *Paul v. Davis*, a case that arose as the result of the publication by the Louisville, Kentucky, police chief of a pamphlet that identified Edward Charles Davis III as an "active shoplifter." Davis had once been arrested but was never tried on the charge that was later dismissed. Chief Paul knew that the publication was false but claimed that there is no difference between arrest and conviction. Davis, prohibited by Kentucky law from suing even for this deliberate defamation, brought a Federal suit for denial of due process. He had been declared guilty without trial. In an opinion written by Justice William Rehnquist, the Supreme Court of the United States denied Davis even this relief on the grounds that he had lost neither liberty nor property as the result of this defamation. Privacy and reputation have no property value. This conclusion was in marked contrast to Rehnquist's position three weeks earlier in *Time v. Firestone*, a case considered in the next chapter, where an unintentional defamation was committed by a news magazine rather than a public official.

Although Rosenbloom was precluded from bringing suit against the original source of his defamation, he could still bring suit against the

broadcaster of the defamation, WIP. In his suit
Rosenbloom noted that WIP had failed to use the
word "allegedly" in the third sentence of its first
two broadcasts of the original story and that the
tone of the second story was insulting and de-
meaning. He also argued that the element of identification was present in the second story even
though he was not mentioned by name because by
that time the radio audience would obviously
know the identity of those involved. He further
claimed that WIP had been negligent, had not
taken the care of the average prudent person, in
preparing its broadcasts. Since George Rosenbloom was not a celebrity or a public official, negligence was the appropriate standard for proving
fault.

WIP rested its defense on four points. The
first was a claim of privilege. Since Captain Ferguson's statements were privileged communication
protected by the principle of sovereign immunity,
WIP's reports of those statements were also protected. Second, WIP had exercised proper care
given the nature of its news operation. It operated
under extreme time pressures with a small staff
and was entirely dependent upon outside sources
for its information. Third, in the second broadcast

Rosenbloom was not identified. Finally, the broadcasts were essentially truthful reports of the information that WIP had received.

The cross examination of WIP witnesses by Rosenbloom's lawyer established that Captain Ferguson had been the source for the first broadcast. In the case of the second broadcast WIP's news director was unable to identify positively any particular source. While he was "sure we would check with the District Attorney's office also and with the Police Department," he also admitted "it would be difficult for me to specifically state what additional corroboration we had."

As the judge explained to its members, the jury that heard Rosenbloom's suit had several tasks. It needed to decide if Rosenbloom had been identified in the broadcasts. It needed to decide if the broadcasts had damaged Rosenbloom's reputation and held him up to public hatred, contempt, or ridicule. It needed to determine whether the reporting was false. Finally, on the question of passing on privileged communication, it was explained that under Pennsylvania law news media could lose that privilege by "'want of reasonable care and diligence to ascertain the truth, before giving currency to an untrue communication.' The failure to employ such 'reasonable care and diligence' can destroy a privilege which otherwise would protect the utterer of the communication."

If the jury decided that WIP had broadcast damaging falsehoods without showing reasonable care, its next task would be to determine damages. General damages could be awarded for loss of business that the jury concluded was the direct result of the broadcasts. On the question of punitive damages the judge gave the jury the following instructions:

> If you find that this publication arose from a bad motive or malice toward the plaintiff, or if you find that it was published with reckless indifference to the truth, if you find that it was not true, you would be entitled to award punitive damages, and punitive damages are awarded as a deterrent from future conduct of the same sort.
>
> They really are awarded only for outrageous conduct, as I have said, with a bad motive or with reckless disregard of the interests of others, and before you would award punitive damages you must find that these broadcasts were published with a bad motive or with reckless disregard of the rights of others or reckless indifference to the rights of others. . . .

After due consideration the jury returned a verdict in favor of George Rosenbloom. It awarded him $25,000 in general damages. The jury also awarded Rosenbloom $725,000 in punitive damages. Given the judge's instructions, the jury must have concluded that WIP had not only been negligent but also had in fact broadcast knowing falsehoods or had shown a reckless disregard for the truth or falsity of what it broadcast. While the size of the punitive award was later reduced to $250,000, the award by 1964 standards was quite substantial, apparently reflecting the jury's perception of the magnitude of WIP's misconduct.

Given the size of the *Rosenbloom* judgment, the appeal by WIP was not unexpected. The United States Third Circuit Court of Appeals ruled in favor of WIP and set aside the trial court's verdict. Following the trend indicated by the Supreme Court of the United States, the appeals court concluded that Rosenbloom's status as a private person was not of "decisive importance" and that he needed to establish the reckless disregard or knowing falsehood standard of fault. Given the hot news-short deadline pressures under which WIP operated, the appeals court concluded that the evidence presented at the trial was insufficient, contrary to the decision reached by the trial jury in awarding punitive damages. Rosenbloom then appealed this reversal to the Supreme Court.

The Supreme Court of the United States heard Rosenbloom's appeal in 1970, slightly more than seven years after the WIP broadcasts in question, and issued a decision the following year. By a vote of five to three the Court sustained the decision of the court of appeals in favor of WIP. However, the five justice majority could not agree on the reasons for the decision. The lead opinion, supported by only two other justices, was written by Justice William Brennan, the author of the Court's opinion in *New York Times v. Sullivan*. In essence Brennan agreed with the appeals court view that the distinction between public and private persons was unimportant. He said,

> If a matter is a subject of public or general interest it cannot suddenly become less so merely because a private individual did not "voluntarily" choose to become involved. . . . We honor the commitment to robust debate on public issues, which is embodied in the First Amendment, by extending constitutional protection to all discussion and communication involving matters of public or general

concern, without regard to whether the persons involved are famous or anonymous.

Since it is logical to assume that no news media would disseminate information that was not "of public or general concern," then Brennan and his two fellow justices, by eliminating the distinction between *public* and *private* persons, were saying that reckless disregard or knowing falsehood is the appropriate level of fault in virtually all defamation cases. Only plaintiffs in cases arising from publication of false stories of no public interest would be exempt from this standard.

The other two justices in the majority did not accept Brennan's reasons for overturning the trial jury's award to Rosenbloom. Justice Hugo Black restated his view that all libel laws are a violation of the First Amendment. Justice Byron White based his decision on the issue of privileged communication and, in essence, argued that Captain Ferguson's privileged communication should extend to WIP's reporting of that communication.

The two opinions written by the three dissenting justices were in general agreement on the major issues presented by the case and explicitly recognized that the Brennan opinion would establish reckless disregard or knowing falsehood as the standard of fault for all defamation suits. While they acknowledged that strict liability was not an appropriate standard of fault, they also insisted that states should be able to apply a negligence standard of fault in defamation cases involving private individuals. They also expressed concern about awards of punitive damages such as the trial jury's $725,000 award to Rosenbloom. Justices Thurgood Marshall and Potter Stewart would prohibit all punitive damage awards, while Justice John Harlan said that such awards were legitimate providing they bore some relationship to actual damages. The question of punitive damages aside, all three recognized that a jury had found Rosenbloom to be the victim of false and defamatory news reports and entitled to compensation for his injury.

These opinions of the Supreme Court left most of the defamation issues raised by the case unresolved. On the central question of fault the three justice plurality opinion for the Court's majority sought to establish the principle that reckless disregard or knowing falsehood would need to be proven in all defamation cases. However, that position was not supported by any of the other justices who participated in the case. A definitive statement about fault and its relationship to the character of the defamation plaintiff had not been provided.

The dissenting opinions included a helpful discussion of the question of damages. On the one hand, the appropriateness of general or compensatory damages was recognized, as was the real difficulty of assessing damages accurately. On the other hand, the appropriateness of assessing punitive damages was questioned. Large awards to punish media misconduct were seen to damage freedom of the press. One justice thought that such awards, while proper in egregious cases, should show some relationship to actual injury. Two other justices would prohibit punitive awards altogether.

The final question posed by the *Rosenbloom* case concerned the role of privileged communication in defamation cases. Justice White acknowledged and supported sovereign immunity and the privilege that flowed from it. However, the rest of the Court did not address this issue. The obvious facts were that George Rosenbloom was improperly arrested by police who did not know the law, and that he was defamed by the reports on and comments about those arrests. But because of the principle of immunity, Rosenbloom could not bring suit against the person responsible for his injury.

In 1979, eight years after the *Rosenbloom* case was decided, the Supreme Court of the United States finally addressed the question of immunity directly in *Hutchinson v. Proxmire*. In this case the Court majority drew a distinction between protected official conduct and nonofficial conduct that is not protected. Official conduct—speeches on the floor of the United States Senate—is protected by explicit privilege stated in the speech and debate clause of Article I of the United States Constitution. However, the Court majority ruled that press conferences and news releases were not protected official communication. A United States senator could be held liable for unofficial utterances. If this distinction between official, privileged communication and unofficial communication lacking any privilege had existed at the time of Rosenbloom's arrest, he might have been able to sue Captain Ferguson for the defamation arising from the unofficial telephone calls to news agencies publicizing the arrest of "a major smut distributor." Those telephone calls, unlike the pamphlet written by Police Chief Paul in the *Paul v. Davis* case, were not part of Captain Ferguson's official duties.

5

The Definitive Definition of a Public Person: *Gertz v. Welch*

One of the most sensitive of all law enforcement issues is dealing with what may appear to be misconduct by law enforcement officials. As we have seen in the case of George Rosenbloom, an officer can defame an innocent person without being held accountable for that action. In Spike Lee's controversial 1989 film *Do the Right Thing*, the denouement of the drama is the murder of the black character Radio Raheem by a white police officer. While those who were upset by this thought-provoking film criticized it for many reasons, few argued that the confrontation Lee presented was unrealistic. Anyone who reads a newspaper regularly can recall numerous stories of fatal confrontations between private citizens and the police of most big cities. Frequently the people involved are young and/or members of minority groups as in the Lee film.

The circumstances of these fatal confrontations are almost always a matter of public controversy. Members of the group from which the victim came, even members who have not witnessed the event, dispute the police version of the event. However, internal investigations by police departments or even grand juries usually find that there was justification for the use of deadly force. On rare occasions an officer is indicted and a trial jury is asked to determine which version of the event appears to be the truth. Because these trials are infrequent and touch on strong community feelings about police, they are issues "of public or general concern" and are usually widely publicized.

In a confrontation in an alley next to a hot dog stand near Wrigley Field in June 1968, Chicago police officer Richard Nuccio, who had served just eighteen months on the force, shot and killed nineteen-year-old Ronald Nelson. Nuccio was indicted for murder, tried, convicted, and sentenced to fourteen years in prison.

As is usual in criminal trials, the prosecution and defense presented the jury with alternative stories about what had happened. Both sides

agreed that Nelson and Nuccio had had other confrontations. The prosecution claimed that because
of fear based on his prior experiences, Nelson ran
when he saw Nuccio, who pursued him down the
alley and shot him. The defense described Nelson
as a hoodlum who led Nuccio down the alley and
threw a knife at him. Nuccio shot in self-defense.
The prosecution argued that the knife introduced
to substantiate this version of events had been
planted. The jury, perhaps persuaded by the fact
that Nelson had been shot in the back from a dis-
tance of some eighty feet, found Nuccio guilty.

After the conviction of Nuccio, Ronald
Nelson's family decided to sue the city of Chicago
and Richard Nuccio for damages resulting from
the killing of their son. To represent them in this
case they retained respected Chicago lawyer Elmer
Gertz, in association with Ralla Klepak.

Another outcome of the Nuccio trial was an
eighteen-page lead article entitled "Frame-Up" in
the April 1969 issue of *American Opinion. American
Opinion* was published by the John Birch Society, a
far right group that considered every president of
the United States after Herbert Hoover to be part
of an international communist conspiracy. The article was written by Alan Stang on the basis of "ex-

tensive research" and an "investigative trip" to Chicago and described the prosecution of Nuccio as part of a Communist plot to undermine effective law enforcement. It included a number of statements about Elmer Gertz:

> The file on Elmer Gertz in Chicago Police Intelligence takes a big Irish cop to lift.
>
> He has been an official of the Marxist League for Industrial Democracy, originally known as the Intercollegiate Socialist Society, which has advocated the violent seizure of our government.
>
> In fact, the only thing Chicagoans need to know about Gertz is that he is one of the original officers, and has been Vice President, of the Communist National Lawyers Guild . . . which probably did more than any other outfit to plan the Communist attack on the Chicago police during the 1968 Democratic Convention.
>
> He was active at the inquest [into Nelson's death].

In addition on page nine of the article there appeared a picture of Gertz with the caption "Elmer Gertz of Red Guild harasses Nuccio."

The basic problem with all these references to Gertz was that they were untrue. The implication that he had a criminal record was false. He had never been a member of either the Marxist League for Industrial Democracy or the Intercollegiate Socialist Society. While he had been a member of the National Lawyers Guild fifteen years earlier, the Guild was neither a Communist organization nor did it have any role in events surrounding the 1968 Chicago Democratic Convention. He was an observer for the family at the Nelson inquest but took no part in it except to ask a few questions. He was neither a Communist nor a member of any Communist organization, nor had he in any way harassed Officer Nuccio. All these false accusations led the normally thick-skinned Gertz to bring a libel suit against Robert Welch, Inc., publisher of *American Opinion,* the John Birch Society magazine.

Elmer Gertz's suit came to trial in Federal District Court in Chicago after the Supreme Court's expansion of the concept of public person in the *Butts* and *Walker* cases but before the *Rosenbloom* decision. In this context the trial court judge faced the problem of deciding whether Gertz was a public or private person. While he was well known in legal circles, the judge discovered that not a single member of the jury recognized Gertz's name and concluded that Gertz could sue as a private person.

The case for Gertz consisted of proving that the statements published by *American Opinion* were false. Typical of the evidence presented to the jury was the testimony of Julius Lucius Echeles, one of the lawyers who had represented Richard Nuccio. Echeles testified that not only was Gertz a lawyer of good character but that he had not participated in any "plot" against Officer Nuccio or the police in general. Evidence was also presented to show that the editors of *American Opinion* had done nothing to check the accuracy of "Frame-Up." After hearing all the evidence, the jury returned a verdict of $50,000 in damages against the magazine and its owners.

As is customary in such cases, lawyers for *American Opinion* filed a motion asking the court to set aside the jury's verdict. After careful consideration the judge agreed because he had concluded that Gertz was involved in a matter of public interest. An outraged Gertz appealed this reversal to the United States Circuit Court of Appeals arguing that the trial judge's reversal was an error and contrary to law. While the court of appeals had Gertz's case under consideration, the Supreme Court of

United States issued its decision and opinions in *Rosenbloom v. Metromedia* case. That decision led a reluctant court of appeals to rule against Gertz. As one of the written opinions in *Gertz v. Robert Welch, Inc.* observed:

> It is with considerable reluctance, however, that I concur. The reluctance is due to my fear that we may have in this opinion pushed through what I consider the outer limits of the first-amendment protection against liability of non-"public figures" in their personal privacy.

When other motions failed, Gertz appealed this decision to the Supreme Court of the United States, which heard oral argument in November 1973 and announced its decision the following June. This Court was somewhat different than the one that had considered the *Rosenbloom* case. Justices Hugo Black and John Harlan had been replaced by Justices Lewis Powell and William Rehnquist, and in fact, Justice Powell wrote the opinion for the five justice majority. Although that opinion had the effect of upholding the decisions of the lower court judges, it cannot be characterized as either for or against Gertz.

Justice Powell's opinion dealt with two separate issues: (1) the public or private character of the plaintiff and (2) the nature of the damage award in the case. On the first of these two issues Powell explicitly rejected the reasoning and conclusion of William Brennan in *Rosenbloom*. While recognizing Brennan's belief that "tension exists between the need for a vigorous and uninhibited press and the legitimate interest in redressing wrongful injury," Powell did not agree with the way Brennan and the two justices who agreed with him had resolved that tension in *Rosenbloom*. To justify a distinction between "public" and "private" persons Powell turned to one of Brennan's central arguments in the Sullivan case:

> The first remedy of any victim of defamation is self-help—using available opportunities to contradict the lie or correct the error and thereby to minimize its adverse impact on reputation. Public officials and public figures usually enjoy significantly greater access to the channels of effective communication and hence have a more realistic opportunity to counteract false statements than private individuals normally enjoy. Private individuals are therefore more

vulnerable to injury, and the state interest in
protecting them is correspondingly greater.

In *Sullivan,* Brennan had used this argument to
support giving less protection to public officials.
Here Powell used it to support more protection for
private persons.

In the case of public persons/public officials
and others who "have thrust themselves to the
forefront of particular public controversies in order
to influence the resolution of the issues involved," — the *Sullivan* standard of fault — reckless
or knowing falsehood — was reaffirmed. On the
other hand, states should be free to require a less
rigorous standard of fault such as negligence for
those who do not meet this public person test. The
rejection of the strict liability standard of fault stated
in *Sullivan* was also reaffirmed. Powell concluded
that Gertz should have been considered a private
person as the trial judge had originally decided.

The second part of Powell's opinion for the
Court majority addressed the issue of damages. In
injury cases such as defamation suits juries can
award several kinds of damages to the successful
plaintiff. An award that is payment for demonstrated direct financial loss is called *special* dam-

ages. Special damages may be awarded to doctors who prove that they lost patients and income as the result of defamatory statements. However, in most defamation cases the injury to reputation at the heart of the suit cannot be represented by specific dollar amounts. In these cases juries may award *general* damages based on their understanding of the real injury to reputation resulting from the defamatory publication. Both special and general damages are sometimes referred to as *compensatory* or *actual* damages because their size and purpose is to compensate the injured party for that injury. In some cases where a jury finds fault but no real injury it might award *nominal* or *token* damages such as the one dollar in compensatory damages awarded to Barry Goldwater in his suit against *fact*. Finally, there are *punitive* damages intended, as their label demonstrates, to punish the publishers of defamation for their acts. Powell's discussion of these various forms of damages is clear and concise:

> [We recognize] the strong and legitimate state interest in compensating private individuals for injury to reputation. But this countervailing state interest extends no fur-

ther than compensation for actual injury. For reasons stated below, we hold that the States may not permit recovery of presumed or punitive damages, at least when liability is not based on a showing of knowledge of falsity or reckless disregard for the truth.

The common law of defamation is an oddity of tort law for it allows recovery of purportedly compensatory damages without evidence of actual loss. . . . Juries may award substantial sums as compensation for supposed damage to reputation without any proof that such harm actually occurred. . . . Additionally, the doctrine of presumed damages invites juries to punish unpopular opinion rather than to compensate individuals for injury sustained by the publication of a false fact. . . .

We need not define "actual injury," as trial courts have wide experience in framing appropriate jury instructions in tort action. Suffice it to say that actual injury is not limited to out-of-pocket loss. Indeed, the more customary types of actual harm inflicted by defamatory falsehood include impairment of reputation and standing in the community, personal humiliation, and mental anguish and suffering. Of course, juries must be limited by appropriate instructions, and all awards must be supported by competent evidence concerning injury, although there need be no evidence which assigns an actual dollar value to the injury. . . .

Punitive damages are wholly irrelevant to the state interest that justifies a negligence standard [of fault] for private defamation actions. They are not compensation for injury. Instead, they are private fines levied by civil juries to punish reprehensible conduct and to deter its future occurrence. In short, the private defamation plaintiff who establishes liability under a less demanding standard than that stated by *New York Times* [*v. Sullivan*—the reckless or knowing falsehood standard] may recover only such damages as are sufficient to compensate him for actual injury.

On this basis the Supreme Court majority vacated the lower court decision against Gertz. While Gertz was a private person who needed to prove only negligence, the jury award was for punitive damages, and Gertz had not established reckless disregard or knowing falsehood. However, Gertz was entitled to a new trial if he wanted one.

While the Court majority spoke in a single clear voice, the four dissenting justices did so for at least four different reasons. Chief Justice Warren

Burger would have reinstated the award to Gertz because lawyers must not be attacked when they represent unpopular causes or clients. Justice William Douglas would have neither supported the award to Gertz nor allowed him to sue again. He argued that the First Amendment clearly prohibited Congress from creating libel laws (and there is no federal libel law). Furthermore, the Fourteenth Amendment making the First Amendment applicable to state laws would therefore prohibit any state libel laws as well. Thus he argued that all libel laws are unconstitutional. Justice Brennan, using the arguments that he had developed in his *Rosenbloom* opinion, repeated his view that all libel plaintiffs must prove reckless disregard or knowing falsehood in order to be awarded damages. He also would have vacated the award to Gertz.

Finally, Justice Byron White, in the longest of the dissenting opinions, took issue with almost every aspect of the majority opinion, labeling its positions as "radical changes in the law and severe invasions of the prerogatives of the States." States should be allowed broad discretion to determine appropriate level of fault, including strict liability, and whatever types of damage awards that they see fit. Except in the case of seditious libel such as

New York Times v. Sullivan, "scant, if any, evidence exists that the First Amendment was intended to abolish the common law of libel, at least to the extent of depriving ordinary citizens of meaningful redress against their defamers." He added, "I fail to see how the quality or quantity of public debate will be promoted by further emasculation of state libel laws for the benefit of the news media". For these reasons he, like Chief Justice Burger, would have reinstated the award to Gertz.

When the *Gertz v. Welch* dust settled, the laws of libel may not have been radically changed as Justice White charged, but they were clarified in the following ways: (1) *Public* persons were public officials and those who "have thrust themselves to the forefront of particular public controversies in order to influence the resolution of the issues involved." All others, including those who are drawn involuntarily into public controversy, were *private* persons. (2) Fault in defamation suits was limited to negligence as a possible standard for private persons while public persons must prove reckless or knowing falsehood. (3) Damage awards were limited to compensation for demonstrated injury. However, punitive damages might be awarded upon proof of reckless or knowing falsehood.

While the rules after *Gertz v. Welch* seemed clear, application of the principles was less clear. In particular, repeated controversies arose over the problem of who was a public person. Because the public person requirement of proof of fault was much more demanding than that for private persons, media defendants were always eager to have courts rule that their accusers were public persons. Thus, it is not surprising that the Supreme Court of the United States found itself faced with a series of cases in which the status of the plaintiff was the central issue. Two cases in particular are significant.

For two years the residents of Palm Beach, Florida, and surrounding areas were regaled with almost unbelievable stories of sexual misconduct as Russell and Mary Firestone bitterly fought each other for divorce. Both charged the other with, among other things, multiple counts of adultery. During this period Mary Firestone held numerous press conferences to make charges against her husband and to comment on his against her. She also subscribed to a press clipping service to keep track of her media exposure. After seventeen months of testimony, the trial court judge granted Russell Firestone a divorce and at the same time awarded Mary Firestone $3,000 a month alimony. *Time* magazine reported this outcome in its "Milestones" column in the 22 December 1967 issue:

> Divorced: By Russell A. Firestone, Jr.
> 41, heir to the tire fortune: Mary Alice Sullivan Firestone, 32, his third wife; a one time
> Palm Beach schoolteacher; on grounds of extreme cruelty and adultery; after six years of
> marriage, one son; in West Palm Beach, Fla.
> The 17-month intermittent trial produced
> enough testimony of extramarital adventures
> on both sides, said the judge, "to make Dr.
> Freud's hair curl."

Although there was ample trial testimony of adultery, the judge's ruling had not specified the grounds on which Russell Firestone's suit had been granted. However, a special feature of Florida divorce law prohibited an award of alimony where adultery is the grounds for divorce. Thus, *Time* had in this brief notice published a false and defamatory statement when it listed adultery as one of the grounds for the divorce, and Mary Firestone sued.

Given the deadline pressures under which *Time* operated, the lack of clarity in the trial judge's decision and opinion, and the technicalities of Florida divorce law of which many lawyers were probably unaware, *Time*'s error would seem at most to be an example of negligence—not taking the care of the average prudent person in preparing the "Milestones" note. There did not appear to be any evidence of reckless or knowing falsehood in connection with the story. Thus, the public or private person status of Mary Firestone was a central issue.

Mary Firestone's libel suit took place in the context of the *Butts* and the *Walker* decisions by the Supreme Court of the United States in which the Court ruled that in addition to public officials, widely known people were required to prove reckless or knowing falsehood in order to win a libel judgment. However, the trial court rejected *Time*'s argument that Mary Firestone belonged in this group of public persons, and the jury awarded Firestone a $100,000 judgment, which was upheld by the Florida appeals and supreme courts.

By the time this case was heard by the Supreme Court of the United States the *Gertz* criteria for determining public persons had been established. *Time* argued that by the *Gertz* rule Mary Firestone was clearly a public person. She filed for divorce in a case that attracted great public interest and attention, had held press conferences, and had so much media attention that she used a clipping service. She had injected herself into a matter of public interest and sought to influence the outcome in her favor.

Justice Rehnquist, writing for the Court majority, reaffirmed the *Gertz* rule that people who "thrust themselves to the forefront of particular public controversies in order to influence the resolution of the issues involved" are public persons. However, in the case of Mary Firestone,

> Respondent did not assume any role of especial prominence in the affairs of society, other than perhaps Palm Beach society, and she did not thrust herself to the forefront of any particular public controversy in order to influence the resolution of issues involved in it.
>
> Petitioner [*Time*] contends that because the Firestone divorce was characterized by the Florida Supreme Court as a "cause celebre," it must have been a public controversy and respondent must be considered a public figure. But in doing so petitioner seeks to equate "public controversy" with all controversies of interest to the public.

Although a divorce may be of public interest, it is a private matter and not a public controversy in the sense of the term used in *Gertz*. Thus, Mary Firestone needed to prove only negligence to win her suit. However, two of the majority justices, Powell and Stewart, expressed strong doubts that there was really sufficient evidence to prove that *Time* had been guilty of negligence in spite of that assertion by the Florida Supreme Court. Because of the technical point that the trial record did not indicate that any specific level of fault had been found, the judgment against *Time* was vacated, and the case was returned to the Florida courts for a retrial that never took place.

In 1974, the same year that the *Gertz* decision was announced, the Reader's Digest Association, a staunchly conservative publishing company, issued *KGB: The Secret Work of Soviet Agents*. The book described alleged Soviet espionage and listed names of those claimed to be Soviet agents in the United States. The footnote explaining the list said that the people named were agents "convicted of espionage or falsifying information or perjury and/or contempt charges following espionage indictments or who fled to the Soviet bloc to avoid prosecution." Included in the list was Ilya Wolston, and the book's index reference to his name said, "Wolston, Ilya, Soviet agent in U.S."

Ilya Wolston sued the Reader's Digest Association for libel. He did not fall into any of the categories listed in the footnote nor had he ever been identified by any law enforcement agency as a Soviet agent. In 1957 and 1958, during an investigation of some of his relatives by the FBI, Wolston had been questioned several times and at one point failed to appear before a grand jury when subpoenaed. He later did testify, and in response to government harassment of his pregnant wife, Wolston agreed to plead guilty of contempt of court and was given a one-year suspended sentence. Wolston's legal problems received attention in the Washington, D.C., and New York City newspapers at the time.

While the Reader's Digest Association admitted that an error had been made, it asked the court to dismiss Wolston's suit on the grounds that he was a public person under the *Gertz* rule and that the error was not a reckless or knowing falsehood. When the trial court granted the motion, Wolston appealed, and in 1979 the Supreme Court of the United States ruled in favor of Wolston. Once again Justice Rehnquist concluded that the

Gertz standard did not apply for two reasons. First, the historical record of the public controversy in which Wolston was involved showed that he had been drawn unwillingly into the controversy rather than having "thrust himself to the forefront of a particular public controversy in order to influence the resolution of the issues involved." Second, even if Wolston might conceivably have been a public person in 1958, he certainly was not a public person in 1974, sixteen years later.

In these two cases Justice Rehnquist's opinions for the Court majority amplified the original *Gertz* rule (that Justice Powell had formulated) and applied the rule to specific cases. The application of the *Gertz* rule would be strict. The subject matter of any purportedly libelous report would need to be a truly public current controversy. Personal privacy would be guarded so that private matters, no matter how great public interest in them might be, would not fall under the *Gertz* rule. Those drawn against their will into public controversies would not as a result become public persons.

Finally, in 1981, Elmer Gertz's suit against *American Opinion* was retried. After hearing the evidence, the jury took less than ninety minutes to come to a conclusion on this case that had begun twelve years earlier. The jury found that *American Opinion* was not only negligent in publishing "Frame-Up" but also had printed knowing false-hoods or shown reckless disregard for the truth or falsity of what it printed. Gertz was awarded $100,000 in compensatory damages and an additional $300,000 in punitive damages. Under the *Gertz* rule this punitive award was allowable because reckless or knowing falsehood had been proven.

6

The Rules of Libel—Beyond Comprehension

At the end of November 1979, *The Washington Post* published a pair of stories written by *Post* reporter Patrick Tyler describing a complex series of business arrangements undertaken by Mobil Oil Company that appeared to have enriched Mobil Oil President William Tavoulareas' son Peter. In 1974 Mobil organized a series of leases of its own tanker, first to a Saudi Arabian corporation and then back to Mobil. To handle these transactions, a London shipping corporation was established with Peter Tavoulareas, a recent college graduate, as a half partner. The company, Atlas Maritime Corporation, did millions of dollars of business with Mobil under exclusive no-bid contracts.

Tyler explored this story as the result of a tip received from another reporter who worked for a small suburban newspaper. He examined the available records of the deal and interviewed many of those involved. Two major sources were Peter's partner in Atlas and an ex-son-in-law of William Tavoulareas who was angry at having been eliminated as a partner in the deal. The story and its evolution illustrate the process of investigative reporting. Reporters take ideas and with the support of their editors conduct the research needed to develop enough information to write the news stories. Unlike stories based on press releases and public events, these stories do not exist prior to the reporters' investigations.

While the stories explained why there were good political and economic reasons for the lease arrangements, the front page headline for the first story read, "Mobil Chief Sets Up Son in Venture." The overall impression that a reader might get was that William Tavoulareas had used his position as president of Mobil to provide special financial benefits for his son Peter. Beyond what might simply be seen as normal business community nepotism, the articles suggested that Securities and Exchange Commission regulations about concealing conflicts of interest may have been violated. In fact, these regulations had not technically been violated because Peter did not live with his father. This error was typical of the few inaccuracies that did appear in the two articles.

Shortly after the articles were published William Tavoulareas met with *Post* Editor Benjamin Bradlee to demand a retraction because what had been published was false and, by suggesting illegal conduct, defamatory. While Bradlee refused to print a retraction, the *Post* did publish another story which presented in full the denial of any wrongdoing by Tavoulareas and Mobil Oil. After making repeated efforts over the next several months to persuade *The Washington Post* to publish a retraction, William and Peter filed a $50 million dollar libel suit against the paper.

In July 1982, a little more than two and a half years after the original stories were published, the Tavoulareas libel suit came to trial in Federal District Court in Washington, D.C., before a six-member jury. The first task of the jury was to determine whether there had been defamation. Had the *Post* fairly presented the facts giving full consideration to all the possible interpretations of fact? If the jury concluded that the articles had been defamatory by falsely accusing the Tavoulareases of illegal activity, the next step would be to determine fault.

In this case the problem of determining the appropriate level of fault in relation to the two plaintiffs was difficult. After due consideration the trial court judge, Oliver Gasch, decided that on the basis of the *Gertz* rule William Tavoulareas was a public person while son Peter was a private person. This ruling meant that the jury would need to find that the *Post* published reckless or knowing falsehoods in regard to William Tavoulareas if he were to be awarded damages. In the case of Peter Tavoulareas, the jury needed only to find negligence, failure to take the care of the average prudent person, in preparing and publishing the stories. As reported by Steven Brill in *The American Lawyer*, Judge Gasch spent about two hours instructing the jurors about the law before they began their deliberations. In the course of these instructions he said:

> It is not the defendants' burden to prove that the articles are true. The burden is upon the plaintiffs to prove to you that they are substantially false. . . .
>
> It is not enough for William Tavoulareas to prove that the defendants did not conduct a thorough investigation of the facts or that they were negligent in the way they wrote or edited the articles. To recover, William Tavoulareas must prove the defen-

> dants had a high degree of awareness that
> the articles were false or probably false and
> that they were recklessly disregarded,
> whether the articles were false or not.

After a three-week trial, the jury deliberated
for three days before reaching a verdict. It concluded that the *Post* articles had been defamatory
and awarded William Tavoulareas $250,000 in
compensatory damages and $1.8 million in puni-
tive damages. Peter Tavoulareas received nothing.
Clearly this decision was both surprising and trou-
blesome. If the jury had applied the law as the
judge had instructed, then it must have concluded
that the *Post* had not been negligent in what it
wrote about Peter while at the same time publishing reckless or knowing falsehoods about William.
Not surprisingly, the *Post* asked Judge Gasch to set
aside the jury's verdict as unwarranted by the evidence or otherwise grant the *Post* a new trial.

The bizarre nature of the jury's verdict
prompted journalist Steven Brill to question the
jurors about their decision. He interviewed five of
the six jurors and found two principal difficulties
in the jury's deliberations. The first difficulty was
that they had, in fact, not clearly understood Judge

Gasch's instructions. One of their first actions had been to request a written copy of those instructions, which the judge, in agreement with the lawyers for both sides, denied. This refusal, common in trials, rests on the idea that the jurors must act on the basis of the total instructions and not just read parts of them. The judge would probably have reread the entire instructions if asked. When Brill asked the jurors if they would have come to the same conclusion if they had known there had to be proof that *The Washington Post* had been recklessly or deliberately inaccurate or unfair, the jurors all agreed they would have decided in favor of the *Post*. Of course, that was precisely the standard that Judge Gasch had instructed them to apply.

The second difficulty Brill detected, as reported in his article in the November 1982 issue of *The American Lawyer,* was that the jury was led astray by their elected foreman, a Library of Congress law reference librarian. Not disclosed in the questioning of prospective jurors was that he was an aspiring lawyer who had been accepted and would be entering Catholic University law school in less than two months. This juror eventually persuaded the others by repeatedly demanding that they show how the *Post* articles proved the charge that William Tavoulareas had "set up" his son Peter. This demand placed the burden of proof on *The Washington Post* even though Judge Gasch's instructions had clearly said that it was the Tavoulareases who needed to prove that the *Post* had made defamatory errors and was at fault.

When the jurors finally decided against *The Washington Post,* it was this same juror that came up with the novel legal notion that because Peter Tavoulareas was a private person, he had no reputation that could be damaged and thus was entitled to nothing. On the other hand, William Tavoulareas was entitled to damages because he was a public person with a public reputation that could be damaged. Of course, this line of reasoning reversed the entire idea of the distinction between public and private persons and the different levels of fault that each must prove. There was nothing in Judge Gasch's instructions to support this reasoning.

In sum, Steven Brill found that the decision in the Tavoulareas suit against *The Washington Post* was the result of deliberations by five jurors who did not understand the law and one who thought he did. They did not understand the distinction in defamation law between public and private persons. They did not understand the different standards for fault—negligence or reckless or knowing falsehood. They did not understand that the plaintiffs and not the defendants had the burden of proof. This lack of understanding and misinformation produced the incomprehensible verdict against *The Washington Post*.

Six months after the publication of Brill's study, Judge Gasch acted favorably on the *Post*'s motion to set aside the jury's verdict. The heart of his ruling was the conclusion that the trial record contained no evidence that the *Post* articles "contained knowing lies or statements made in reckless disregard of the truth." One juror interviewed by *The New York Times* for a story published 5 May 1983 expressed elation that the Judge had overturned the jury's "bad decision." This juror also affirmed the accuracy of Brill's report in *The American Lawyer*.

The ruling by Judge Gasch did not, however, end the case. William Tavoulareas, noting that the jury had found the *Post* articles false and defamatory, appealed Judge Gasch's ruling to the Fourth Circuit Court of Appeals, which accepted the case and issued a decision in April 1985 reinstating the jury's award. While the case was being considered by the Court of Appeals, Mobil placed a series of editorial advertisements, published on the "Op-Ed" page of *The New York Times* and in many other leading magazines and newspapers, criticizing libel law in the United States. One typical ad reprinted a speech to Mobil stockholders by William Tavoulareas in which he said that the *Sullivan* rule "meant that the press could print lies about our leaders and remain free from any liability" and called for removal of the reckless disregard or knowing falsehood standard of fault. Of course, what the *Sullivan* decision said was that while the press can make mistakes without fault, it may be punished if it lies.

To many observers the rambling, eighty-eight page opinion written by appeals court Judge George MacKinnon in *Tavoulareas v. Washington Post Co.* was fully as bizarre as the original jury verdict. Judge MacKinnon, joined by Judge Antonin Scalia (now a United States Supreme Court Justice), concluded that there was sufficient evidence in the trial court record to prove that *The Washington Post* had published knowing or reckless falsehoods. After observing that such conclusions are inherently subjective, Judge MacKinnon went on to find circumstantial evidence of reckless or knowing falsehood because the *Post* was known for "hard-hitting investigative stories." In other words it can be assumed that investigative reporting involves the publication of reckless or knowing falsehoods.

As might be expected, this decision and opinion were met by shock and dismay. In his dissenting opinion appeals court Judge J. Skelly Wright commented:

> If this excessive jury verdict on these mundane, flimsy facts is upheld, the effect on freedom of expression will be incalculable. The message to the media will be unmistakable—steer clear of unpleasant news stories and comments about interests like Mobil or pay the price.

Judge Wright was joined by magazine and newspaper editors across the country in observing that the majority opinion reflected a climate of hostility against the press. What most people in the business would view as good journalistic practice was now being used as evidence of publication of reckless or knowing falsehoods.

On a motion by *The Washington Post* the judges of the court of appeals agreed by a vote of ten to two to rehear the case. Judge MacKinnon, ignoring the arguments to the contrary, particularly the Brill study of the trial jury, defended his position as reported in the 12 June 1985 issue of *The New York Times:* "This is a case where the record demonstrates that a properly instructed jury found liability and that it was improper for the trial court to reweigh the jury's finding on credibility."

In October 1985 oral argument was held before a nine-judge panel of the Fourth Circuit Court of Appeals. Edward Bennett Williams, representing *The Washington Post,* argued that the appeals court had an obligation to look at the entire case record—both the law and the facts. *The New York Times* of 4 October 1985 reported that at one point he observed, "Anyone who believes that [Peter Tavoulareas] a $14,000-a-year clerk went to a 75 percent ownership of Atlas on the basis of meritocracy has to believe in the tooth fairy." John J. Walsh, representing William Tavoulareas, argued that the jury's determination of the facts should not be subject to reexamination by appellate courts. This *Times* story also stated that one judge, noting the complexity of the instructions to the jury, asked the key question, "How could ordinary

mortals be asked to retain that during deliberations?" The only answer that attorney Walsh could
offer was that Judge Gasch had given full and legally sound instructions.

In March 1987, seventeen months after hearing the oral arguments and almost eight years after publication of the original articles, the court of
appeals issued its decision and opinion. By a vote
of seven to one the court ruled in favor of *The
Washington Post*. The majority opinion, written
jointly by Judges Kenneth W. Starr and J. Skelly
Wright, contained the following observations:

> [W]e have at every turn accepted only undis-
> puted factors or Tavoulareas's version of dis-
> puted facts, avoiding any evaluations of
> credibility and credited all permissible infer-
> ences the jury may have drawn favorably to
> the Tavoulareas's. Having done so, we none-
> theless are constrained to conclude that the
> evidence is insufficient to constitute clear
> and convincing evidence of actual malice
> [the legal label for reckless or knowing false-
> hoods].

In his dissenting opinion Judge George MacKinnon stated that in his view the trial record "consti-

tutes clear and convincing proof that the *Post* article was published with reckless disregard of its
truth or falsity, and the jury's verdict should be reinstated."

Both the majority and the dissenting opinions of the court of appeals firmly agreed that it is
appropriate for appellate courts to review the trial
facts in defamation cases. The two opinions were
based on different interpretations of the facts rather than a disagreement about the law. The majority opinion implied that the jury had incorrectly
interpreted the facts because it did not understand
the law. However, the key question asked in oral
argument—How can ordinary mortals retain complex defamation law instructions during deliberations?—was not explicitly answered.

News stories about *Tavoulareas v. The Washington Post* reported that William Tavoulareas
spent over $2 million in legal fees pursuing his
case. Most observers agree that *The Washington
Post* spent at least as much. A substantial portion
of these costs arose from the appeals process. In
sum, a great deal of money was expended because
a trial jury did not understand the complexities of
the laws of libel at the time of the trial as explained by the trial court judge.

Although the process was costly, the eventual outcome of the Tavoulareases' suit against *The Washington Post* was a satisfactory one for the news media defendant; the *Post* was financially strong enough to pay the high cost of its eventual vindication. Unfortunately, not all results of misguided jury deliberations are corrected, as *Green v. Alton Telegraph* demonstrates.

On a much smaller scale than *The Washington Post*, the *Alton Telegraph* had a reputation in its community and throughout Illinois for responsible and significant investigative reporting. Over the years the paper had reported a variety of cases of crime and corruption that might otherwise not have come to light. The reporters and editors of this family newspaper shared a commitment to expose the plentiful wrongdoing in their suburban St. Louis community.

In 1968 two *Alton Telegraph* reporters, Joe Melosi and William Lhotka, began to explore what seemed to them to be a curious relationship between a local savings and loan bank, a major local contractor, and several people with supposed organized crime connections. Robert DeGrand, Vice-President of the Piasa First Federal Savings and Loan Association of Alton, had approved a large number of construction loans to Jim Green, a major local contractor with close business ties to Donald Hazel, a man with a significant criminal record and supposed organized crime connections. Among the many questions the reporters sought to answer were the following: Were the banking practices of the savings and loan association sound?, Was the bank being used to launder Chicago Mafia money?, Was the bank providing special benefits to the construction company?, Were organized crime figures hidden partners in the construction company?, and Who were the real owners of the apartment houses that the construction company built?

The effort to answer these questions led reporters Melosi and Lhotka to examine the public records of deeds and land transfers and to interview those who might have information, including local law enforcement investigators. This research established that Green was in fact receiving special treatment. The bank had loaned him six times more money than was permitted under federal savings and loan regulations. Hazel owned a lot of what Green was building. The law enforcement people told Melosi and Lhotka that Mafia money was going into Piasa Savings and Loan, but they offered no evidence other than their assertions of this fact.

While the *Alton Telegraph* published stories on financial connections that had been discovered and could be documented, Melosi and Lhotka turned to federal investigators to confirm or deny the central issue of the Mafia connection. They contacted two Justice Department attorneys that they knew, Brian Conboy and David Martin, with whom they agreed to share information in exchange for advance information if anything should be discovered. At the end of March 1969, in a memo to Brian Conboy marked "confidential" on every page, Joe Melosi summarized all that the two reporters had discovered. The memo reported the tips regarding the Mafia connection as well as the fact that these tips were unsubstantiated.

When Brian Conboy left the Justice Department a short time later, he left the "confidential" memo behind. The memo was reviewed by others in the department who suggested to the Federal Home Loan Bank Board (FHLBB) that it might be well to audit the records of Piasa Savings and Loan with great care. That audit quickly revealed the improper loans to Green, and any additional lending was prohibited. Eventually Robert DeGrand

was dismissed as Piasa vice-president; the bank itself was taken over by the Federal Savings and
Loan Insurance Corporation; and the Green construction empire collapsed.

During the time the investigators from the
FHLBB were working at Piasa Savings and Loan,
they made numerous references to their work as a
follow-up on a Justice Department memo although
no one at FHLBB had actually seen the Melosi
memo. However, these hints led both Robert De-
Grand and Jim Green to seek legal assistance to
discover if there were any grounds to sue someone
for compensation for the injury that resulted from
the termination of their financial arrangements.
Through the use of Freedom of Information Act
requests, DeGrand's lawyer uncovered a paper trail
from the Justice Department to the Federal Home
Loan Bank Board that led to the Piasa audit. In response to a request from Green's lawyer, Joe Melosi provided a copy of his original memo. Armed
with this information both men sued for libel
naming as defendants not only Joe Melosi and
William Lhotka but also their employer, the *Alton
Telegraph*.

The first of these suits, *Green v. Alton Telegraph,* came to trial at the end of April 1980, more

than eleven years after Joe Melosi had written his "confidential" memo to Brian Conboy. The trial judge was Charles Chapman, a political appointee who had just lost a judicial election in which he failed to secure the endorsement of the *Alton Telegraph*. Throughout the trial on matters of evidence and law Judge Chapman consistently ruled against the *Alton Telegraph*. Typical of these rulings was Chapman's decision that Green could be awarded damages for injury to his construction company in addition to any possible personal injury. This ruling was clearly contrary to Illinois law. He also ruled that since the paper was aware of its reporters' investigation and the Melosi memo (even though none of the paper's owners or managers had ever seen it), it could be held responsible for the contents of that memo.

The panel of prospective jurors was drawn from surrounding middle class and blue collar areas, and Green's lawyer used his challenges to remove everyone with more than a high school education from the jury. Two of the twelve jurors had never attended high school.

In the trial before this unfriendly judge and less than knowledgeable jury, the case for the defendants did not go well. Judge Chapman's lengthy and complex instructions dealt with not only the meaning of the laws of libel but also with issues such as qualified privilege and the liability of one party (the *Alton Telegraph*) for the damaging actions of another (The Federal Home Loan Bank Board). The jury received the case at 5:00 P.M. and, with time out for dinner, returned a judgment against the *Alton Telegraph* of $9.2 million, substantially more than the total worth of the paper, just five hours later. This award was the largest award in the history of United States libel litigation.

To discover how this verdict happened, Thomas Littlewood interviewed jurors and reported what he found in *Coals of Fire*. He found that the tired and impatient jurors apparently never discussed the judge's instructions or their meaning or application to the case. They never looked at any of the eighty exhibits, some quite lengthy, that they were given to consider. Without vote or any formal determination of responsibility of the *Alton Telegraph*, there was general agreement that Jim Green should get something. The issue after dinner was simply how much to award. In a community known for excessive jury awards, some wanted to award as much as $20 million while others argued for a much smaller amount. Someone suggested and the rest of the jurors agreed, incorrectly, that any punitive award would go to the school district rather than Green. They further agreed that the paper was wealthy and could easily afford whatever award they assessed. The result of these attitudes and ideas was $6.7 million in compensatory damages (only $350,000 less than the total that Green had requested) and $2.5 million in punitive damages. There was no review of the evidence to determine guilt or the presence of knowing or reckless falsehood needed to award punitive damages under the *Gertz* rule.

If there were ever a jury award that should be reversed on appeal it was this $9.2 million award against the *Alton Telegraph*. Judge Chapman had made numerous reversible errors in his trial rulings and instructions to the jury. The jury's award was obviously excessive and lacked any basis in the evidence presented during the trial. However, rules for appeal in Illinois require that defendants who appeal a civil damage award must post a bond equal to one and a half times the damage award before the case can go forward. The *Alton Telegraph* lacked the resources to post the $13.8 million bond needed to make the appeal that would surely have led to a reversal of this tragic miscarriage of justice.

To prevent Jim Green from seizing the paper, the *Alton Telegraph* filed for protection under the bankruptcy laws. After extended negotiations in bankruptcy court and out, the several parties to libel actions against the *Telegraph* agreed to a settlement of about $1.5 million to be paid by the paper and its insurance company. In addition the *Telegraph* paid over $600,000 in legal fees. The *Alton Telegraph* emerged from bankruptcy, was sold to a newspaper chain, and is no longer known for its investigative reporting.

In the *Washington Post* case the jury did not understand the judge's full and careful instructions. It eventually accepted one juror's incorrect understanding of the law. In the *Alton Telegraph* case the judge's faulty instructions were apparently completely ignored by the jury that was interested only in giving the plaintiff some money. Both cases highlight a major difficulty with defamation litigation: juries are unable or unwilling to understand and apply the complex rules for determining fault for a media defendant and awarding appropriate damages once fault has been established. The lengthy series of jury awards that have been reversed on appeal provides documentary evidence of this problem. A typical example is the suit by Kimerli Jayne Pring against *Penthouse* magazine for a piece of sexual fantasy fiction about an imaginary Miss Wyoming in a Miss America contest. A Wyoming jury awarded her $1.5 million in actual damages and $25 million in punitive damages, all of which was reversed on appeal.

The appeals process is not, however, an adequate solution for the problem of a jury that does not or does not choose to understand the law and how it should be applied to the facts of a given case. As the *Alton Telegraph* case illustrates, rules of law can create a situation where a media defendant is prevented from pursuing the appeals that would lead to a reversal. Even in situations where major media defendants such as *Penthouse* or *The Washington Post* have the resources to pursue appeals, the cost of such litigation represents an unnecessary and undesirable burden. This situation has led to a number of proposals to change the way in which defamation controversies are resolved. Some of these proposals will be considered in chapter 8.

7

Defamation Suits as Political Tools: Generals Westmoreland and Sharon

After months of hearing official reports that the Vietnam War was being won and would soon end, the American public was shocked by what came to be called the Tet Offensive that began the last day of January 1968. North Vietnamese forces launched attacks throughout the country including an assault on the United States Embassy in what was then called Saigon. While military experts still argue about whether the offensive was a victory or a defeat for the North Vietnamese, images of the offensive brought home in living color by television had a profound effect on the United States public. The basic question was simply this: If we were winning and the war was almost over, how could such an offensive have happened? The Tet Offensive increased public distrust of official pronouncements and expanded the opposition to continued United States participation in the war.

Even after the signing of a peace treaty and the United States' withdrawal from Vietnam, the question demanded an answer because Tet had clearly been one of the pivotal events of the Vietnam War. One answer to the question was developed in 1975 in an article in *Harper*'s magazine by Sam Adams, a former analyst for the Central Intelligence Agency. Adams argued that the military leadership in Vietnam had deliberately misled both the United States political leadership and the general public about the military strength of the Vietnamese opposition. This idea was investigated and developed by a Columbia Broadcasting System news team and resulted in the CBS News broadcast, "The Uncounted Enemy: A Vietnam Deception," that was broadcast in January 1982, almost exactly fourteen years after the Tet Offensive. That documentary placed the United States commander in Vietnam at the time, General William Westmoreland, at the center of a conspiracy to conceal enemy troop strength.

Although he knew of the planned program and had been interviewed in the process of its preparation, General Westmoreland was angered by the broadcast and made his displeasure known to CBS. Since the General was a prominent public official, he would need to prove that CBS had broadcast reckless or knowing falsehoods, the public person standard of fault established by the Supreme Court of the United States in *New York Times v. Sullivan,* to sue CBS successfully. Lawyers contacted by Westmoreland advised him that because there was no indication that CBS had deliberately used such falsehoods, there was little chance of winning a defamation suit against CBS and a strong likelihood that a judge would dismiss the suit before it came to trial.

Four months after the broadcast, the right-wing weekly *TV Guide* published an article by Don Kowet and Sally Bedell that was highly critical of CBS and the manner in which CBS had prepared the "Uncounted Enemy" documentary. CBS responded to this attack and Westmoreland's complaint by offering the General fifteen minutes of prime, unedited air time to respond to the original documentary in any way he wished. This unprecedented offer was refused by General Westmoreland who demanded that CBS broadcast its own full and complete apology. CBS refused.

Following the *TV Guide* article, representatives of Richard Mellon Scaife, a major financial supporter of radical right causes, and the Scaife Family Charitable Trust contacted Dan M. Burt of the Capital Legal Foundation to ask Burt and Capital to represent General Westmoreland in a libel suit against CBS. Arrangements were made to put Burt in touch with Westmoreland, which produced an agreement to sue CBS. Scaife eventually provided over $2 million of the more than $3 million in Capital's legal fees and costs. The remainder came from the Olin Foundation, Smith Richardson Foundation, and other smaller, far right contributors. Westmoreland's $120 million suit against CBS was filed in September 1982.

The two years between the filing of the suit and the beginning of the trial in Federal District Court in New York City were filled with the usual discovery activities that precede a defamation trial. In addition to taking testimony from people at CBS involved in the preparation of the program, Westmoreland's lawyers sought copies of all film and written material created in the process of making the documentary. Even after the Westmoreland team had gathered all this information, the CBS lawyers felt that there was no case and asked the judge, Pierre Leval, to dismiss the complaint. One motion reported in *The New York Times* of 24 May 1984, claimed that "the statements in the program about which the plaintiff complains are true beyond any genuine dispute of material fact." Judge Leval denied this motion as well as a similar one three months later that noted that the Westmoreland team had been unable to present any evidence that CBS had broadcast reckless or knowing falsehoods.

The trial of *Westmoreland v. CBS* began on 9 October 1984 and was terminated on 18 February 1985—a period of four months, which included a Christmas break. As had been anticipated, the trial became a major media event receiving widespread daily news coverage. The daily presence of CBS and Westmoreland public relations people who provided background and perspective to reporters was evidence of the importance of this coverage to both sides.

The basic case presented for Westmoreland was an effort to persuade both the jury and the general public that CBS had been unfair to him in the production of the disputed documentary. Following the line taken in the *TV Guide* article by Kowet and Bedell two years earlier, Capital Legal Foundation's chief lawyer Dan Burt explored the editorial techniques used in the program prepara-

tion. The idea was to create the impression that
the ordinary techniques of television program
preparation, not commonly known or understood
by the public at large, were inherently biased or
unfair. Extensive testimony was offered about the
way interviews were edited and pieces of film
were juxtaposed to enhance impact on the viewer.
The principal difficulty with this approach was
that while it might produce unfavorable public
perceptions of CBS and broadcast journalism in
general, it did not produce the required proof of
reckless or knowing falsehood on the part of CBS.

Fundamentally, the case for the CBS motion
for dismissal of Westmoreland's suit was that the
statements claimed by Westmoreland to be defamatory were true. David Boies, the attorney representing CBS, began to build this case in cross-
examination of the witnesses who testified on behalf of General Westmoreland. These witnesses
were repeatedly forced to admit that under the
general's direction, real troop strength of the
North Vietnamese had been concealed. When CBS
began to present its own witnesses, the situation
for the general became even worse. Day after day
these witnesses, including some who had been
staff officers for General Westmoreland in Viet-

nam, testified that the central charge of the CBS broadcast was true. A policy had been established to report North Vietnamese troop strength under an arbitrary ceiling of 300,000, regardless of actual intelligence estimates that were at times twice as much.

While the trial's thirty-sixth witness, Westmoreland staff officer Colonel Gains B. Hawkins, was testifying for CBS, Westmoreland's attorney Dan Burt negotiated with the CBS legal staff to reach a settlement. On Monday, 19 February 1985, a settlement agreement was concluded. In exchange for a statement from CBS affirming General Westmoreland's patriotism, which had never been questioned in either the disputed broadcast or the trial, the General dropped all claims against CBS. In addition, CBS agreed not to sue Westmoreland for the legal costs incurred as a result of the suit. The estimate of these costs exceeded $4 million. Given the absence of any factual basis for this defamation suit, a counterclaim for legal costs was a strong possibility.

Understanding defamation litigation in the United States requires an effort to understand the reasons for this costly and meritless defamation suit. A central clue can be found in the constellation of far right individuals and groups who urged General Westmoreland to file the suit and who also paid the legal costs of the suit. These sources had two motives. The first was a simple desire to punish CBS through the expenses of the litigation. The hope was that these costs would discourage CBS from undertaking any new programming critical of important right-wing people.

The second, more complex, motive was an effort to refight the Vietnam War. Radical right mythology includes the belief that the United States news media were responsible for losing the war. The claim is that biased reporting turned the United States public against the war that would have been won if the military had been given a free hand to pursue it. The Tet Offensive was a landmark event in this scenario, and CBS a major villain. Unfortunately for this view, the trial testimony provided further evidence that the war was actually lost on the ground in Vietnam as well as in Washington, D.C.

Given these motives it was not surprising that many of General Westmoreland's supporters were upset about the outcome of the trial. It was obviously unacceptable to credit the decision to abandon the suit to General Westmoreland, who may have realized that his position was hopeless or even that he was being used by his right-wing "friends." Another villain had to be found, and that villain turned out to be the general's principal lawyer, Dan Burt. The clearest example of this scapegoating was the two-part article by Renata Adler in *The New Yorker*, later turned into the book *Reckless Disregard*. Through highly selective use of trial testimony, depositions, and documents Adler attempted to re-establish news media as responsible for losing the Vietnam War and to prove that CBS had shown reckless disregard for the truth in preparing "The Uncounted Enemy." Because the trial outcome supported neither of these positions, Adler justified her position by blaming Dan Burt. According to Adler, it was Dan Burt's inexperience and incompetence rather than the facts that led to the trial outcome.

Given the fact that there was never any evidence to indicate that CBS had broadcast reckless or knowing falsehoods, trial judge Pierre Leval's refusal to act favorably on the CBS motions to dismiss the case is puzzling. Such a dismissal, called summary judgment, would have saved CBS much time and effort as well as money even if General Westmoreland had appealed that judgment, as he might have. Summary judgment is a common, useful tool for disposing of meritless civil suits. Some people have argued that the trial was useful and that a summary judgment would have been seen by the radical right as further evidence of news media conspiracies against "the truth." However, even the trial evidence failed to change the radical right views because they are ideologically determined rather than based on fact.

By coincidence a second defamation trial was taking place in the federal courthouse in New York City while the Westmoreland trial was in progress. This second trial pitted former Israeli Defense Minister Ariel Sharon against the publishers of *Time* magazine. At issue was a single sentence in a cover story about General Sharon that *Time* had published following Israel's invasion of Lebanon in 1982. Sharon had planned and had the final command authority over this invasion that drove more than sixty miles through the southern half of Lebanon, eventually reaching the capital, Beirut. During their occupation of Beirut, Israeli troops allowed Lebanese fascist militia to enter two Palestinian refugee camps and even fired flares to provide light while hundreds of the refugees were murdered.

News of this massacre at the Sabra and Shatila refugee camps shocked the world. Questions
were immediately raised about why the Israeli
army, with complete control of the area, had allowed the militia into the camps and permitted the
killings to take place. Many news reports at the
time suggested that the attack had been permitted
in order to produce panic among the Palestinians.
The public outcry led the government of Israel to
appoint a special commission to investigate the
atrocity. This group, known as the Kahan Commission, issued a report that clearly and explicitly
stated that Ariel Sharon, as the commander of the
Israeli forces, bore direct moral responsibility for
the massacres. The cover story of *Time*'s 21 February 1983 issue reported at length the findings of
the Kahan Commission. Included in that report
was this sentence: "Sharon also reportedly discussed with the Gemayels [leaders of the fascist
militia] the need for the Phalangists to take revenge for the assassination of Bashir, but the details of the conversation are not known." Simply
stated, this sentence suggested that Sharon had
invited these forces to undertake the massacre.
Within days Sharon filed a libel suit in Israel and

later filed a $50 million suit in federal district court in New York City.

Time's initial response was to move that the case be dismissed because Ariel Sharon was "libel proof." To receive a judgment a libel plaintiff must show injury, damage. *Time* argued that the Kahan Commission report had so completely discredited Sharon that his public reputation could not be further harmed. Because the point of Sharon's suit was clearly an effort to salvage his reputation, his attorney, Milton Gould, argued forcefully against this motion. He pointed out that beyond the findings of the Kahan Commission the article suggested that Sharon had "actively encouraged the tragic event." Eventually the court denied *Time*'s motion.

On 13 November 1984, about a month after the start of the Westmoreland trial, the *Sharon v. Time, Inc.* trial began. This trial was an even greater public relations event than *Westmoreland v. CBS*. Outside of court Ariel Sharon accused *Time* of "blood libel" and claimed that the article about him was "one of the most terrible things that has been done to the Jewish people." This statement and others containing thinly veiled charges of anti-Semitism were designed to cloud and confuse the issues in the public mind.

Through his rulings and instructions during the trial itself, Judge Abraham Sofaer kept the trial jury focused on the real issues: Was the disputed sentence in the *Time* article untrue? And if it was untrue, did *Time* publish a reckless or knowing falsehood? *Time* responded to these real issues by presenting evidence showing that to the best of its knowledge the sentence was true. Supporting documentation was said to appear in a secret appendix to the Kahan Commission report. *Time* reporter David Halevy had received information from confidential sources about the contents of the secret appendix reporting Sharon's conversation with the Gemayel family. Halevy's report had been reviewed by *Time* editors, and after Halevy had rechecked the information with his sources, who he testified were reliable, the sentence was included in the *Time* article. Because neither Halevy nor anyone else at *Time* had access to the secret appendix, the *Time* editors trusted their reporter who in turn trusted his sources.

Prior to and throughout the trial, *Time* repeatedly requested that the Israeli government allow examination of the secret appendix, and these requests were refused even though this material was of critical importance to the case. Finally, toward the end of January 1985 while the Westmoreland case was still in progress and just before the Sharon case went to the jury, an agreement was reached to allow trial court Judge Sofaer to examine the appendix and report its contents to the jury. Judge Sofaer told the jury that the appendix did not contain the reported conversation between Sharon and the Gemayels. Given this information the jury easily found that the disputed sentence had been false and defamatory. However, following Judge Sofaer's very careful instructions, the jury also found no evidence that *Time* had been reckless or had published a knowing falsehood.

Although he had lost his $50 million libel suit, Ariel Sharon claimed that he had received complete vindication by the jury's verdict. This claim, like the trial itself, was an obvious effort to direct public attention away from the fundamental truth of Sharon's moral responsibility for the Sabra and Shatila massacres. As Leon Wieseltier commented in the 30 January 1985 issue of *The New York Times*:

> His libel suit was directed not merely against the falsehood of *Time* but also against the

truth of the Kahan Commission. His objective was to wash away the stain that the commission had placed on him, to undo one of the most exemplary exercises of Israeli democracy. He also intended to advance himself in the struggle for the leadership of the Likud [Israel's right-wing political party], where the politics of resentment play very well.

Closer to Sharon's home Hirsh Goodman observed about this verdict in the *Jerusalem Post* of 25 January:

> You have proven that one sentence in one paragraph pertaining to one incident was a lie, but you have yet to prove that you know the meaning of the word "truth." For the truth and you are diametrically opposed. . . . You are not defending me, my country or my people by trying to discredit the system that keeps Israel democratic and those who have been entrusted with power honest.

Although these observers and many others recognized the questionable motives underlying the Sharon suit, such recognition would not restore the millions that *Time* had been forced to spend defending itself.

In addition to having the trials take place at the same time in the same courthouse, the Westmoreland and Sharon cases shared other more significant features. First, both generals were public people according to the criteria established in *Gertz v. Welch*. In order to win a suit both needed to prove that the media defendants had published reckless or knowing falsehoods. In both cases no evidence of such fault existed. In fact, General Westmoreland had been advised that a suit against CBS would be futile.

Second, both suits were used by the plaintiffs and their supporters for purposes other than securing a jury award. In the Westmoreland case the general's supporters had two goals. The first goal was to rewrite history to place responsibility for the loss of the Vietnam War on the news media. The second goal was to punish CBS by forcing it to engage in extensive and expensive litigation. The virulent hostility toward the news media by those on the political radical right fueled this effort.

While Ariel Sharon was seeking to repair damage to his reputation, the traditional motive for a defamation suit, much more was involved. Traditional defamation plaintiffs want a jury to find that damaging untruths were published and to compensate them for the injury. Sharon's actions and the investigation and report on them by an official Israeli commission were the sources that led him to be labeled in many news reports as "The Butcher of Beirut." The disputed erroneous sentence in the *Time* article on the Kahan Commission report offered Sharon an opportunity to cloud the real issue of his moral responsibility for the Sabra and Shatila camp massacres and cater to general public suspicion of the news media. Although the reaction to the outcome of his suit indicates that he was not successful in this attempt, it did help him to continue to play an important role in Israeli politics.

The fundamental fact that emerges from both these cases is that neither suit should have been filed. If filed, neither should have been allowed to come to trial. Both complaints should have been dismissed through the process of summary judgment in favor of the defendants. Neither case was about the traditional goals of a defamation suit to restore injured reputation and receive compensation for the injury inflicted. These two suits cost the parties involved a combined total of well over $10 million, money that surely could have been used in a far more productive manner.

8

What to Do about Defamation

News stories about someone suing someone
else for defamation appear almost daily. Nearly as
frequent are the articles and editorials that deplore
the state of libel litigation in the United States. No
one appears to be satisfied with the laws and the
way they have been interpreted by the courts. Defamation suits are used by people with economic
or political power to harass, intimidate, and punish news media for reporting unpleasant or unflat-
tering but usually truthful news. In other cases
people who actually have been wronged are denied compensation for the injury. Small media defendants often lack the means to defend
themselves successfully against meritless suits,
and protection from the judgments of confused,
misguided, or even hostile juries is clearly inadequate.

Those who speak in support of news media
note with dismay the frequency of defamation
suits and particularly the tendency of juries to ren-

der huge money judgments in favor of plaintiffs. The average defamation award is greater than awards for either product liability or medical malpractice—cases that usually involve actual physical injury and pain. Even though the overwhelming majority of these awards are reduced or completely eliminated on appeal, the costs of the litigation remain. Thus media representatives complain that present laws do not work, that the media need greater protection. Some even argue that the First Amendment requires absolute immunity from defamation suits, the position suggested by Justice Hugo Black in *New York Times v. Sullivan* in 1964 and amplified in *Rosenbloom v. Metromedia* in 1970.

On the other hand, critics of the news media see present defamation rules as unfair to those who are victims of defamation. According to this view, the courts have improperly erected barriers that keep the public from holding the news media accountable and responsible for incompetent or malicious reporting. These antimedia attitudes can become organized campaigns on the political far right by groups such as the misnamed Accuracy in Media. The aim of AIM is to criticize and harass news organizations with the apparent purpose of inhibiting the reporting of news and views with which AIM does not agree. While these efforts may not be directly successful, the repeated loud complaints do have a secondary effect of undermining the credibility of news media with the general public. This weakened credibility contributes to the climate that produces multimillion dollar libel judgments against the media.

Given this widespread dissatisfaction with defamation law, the many voices calling for reform are not surprising. A broad variety of changes and "improvements" have been suggested ranging from demands for a return to the strict liability standard of fault for all to calls for the Supreme Court of the United States to declare that all defamation suits are unconstitutional violations of the First Amendment. While there is agreement that something needs to be done, as the cases reported in the previous chapters have demonstrated, there is no agreement about what should be done. Reviewed here are some of the more interesting and realistic suggestions.

In *Speech and Law in a Free Society* Franklyn S. Haiman proposes that defamation disputes might be resolved by a codified right to reply. This idea rests upon Haiman's basic premise that the best way to deal with bad communication is through more communication. Thus, when false and defamatory information is published, the victim of the defamation should be given a right to reply, an opportunity to set the record straight. No damage suit could be filed unless the opportunity to reply were denied. Returning to the example with which this book began, the first desire of most victims of defamation is to have the error corrected, to have the record set straight.

In spite of its seeming logic, Haiman's proposal has not proven popular with many people concerned with defamation. The political right rejects the idea because it would preclude the opportunity to punish the purportedly liberal media through massive litigation costs and defamation judgments. Neither is this proposal popular with news media representatives who object to losing any of their complete media content control. Perhaps reflecting a siege mentality resulting from repeated right-wing attacks, news media see the surrender of any control as undermining their freedom of expression rights. Given a choice between required media access and being sued, many would rather be sued.

The question of media access required by law was considered by the Supreme Court of the United States in 1974 in *Miami Herald v. Tornillo*. At issue in this case was a Florida law that guaranteed a right to reply to candidates for political office who had been criticized. When the *Miami Herald* refused to give candidate Tornillo an opportunity to reply to a critical editorial, he sued, and the Florida courts found that the *Miami Herald* had violated the law. The paper appealed that decision to the Supreme Court of the United States which found the Florida law with its legal requirement of access an unconstitutional infringement of the First Amendment.

One of the most extensive and systematic studies of the problems of defamation is the Iowa Libel Research Project. The Project is a multiyear examination of actual defamation suits. Some of the results of this study have been reported in *Libel Law and the Press* by Randall P. Bezanson, Gilbert Cranberg, and John Soloski. The cases discussed in their book illustrate the many problems with present law. These analyses demonstrate that while the typical plaintiff often seeks a retraction and/or correction of what has been published rather than any monetary damages, the legal system does not promote the achievement of such ends. Unlike the plaintiff in the hypothetical example with which this book began, the average libel plaintiff does not want to sue, but the system offers no other real options. The often long, difficult, and expensive process of litigation is not really designed to yield a definitive conclusion about the truth or falsity of a published statement even though that is what the average defamation plaintiff wants. Rather, the system encourages pursuit of financial judgment as a second-best substitute.

Given the fact that "the law of libel seems to have disturbingly little relationship to the real actions and objectives of the parties" in libel suits, Bezanson, Cranberg, and Soloski suggest exploration of nonlitigation alternatives to such suits. Programs in arbitration of disputes, fact-finding, and conflict resolution provide models for alternatives in which the goal would be to determine the truth of the disputed published matter. While such a finding would have value, it would only partially satisfy the plaintiff who also seeks restoration of public reputation. Thus any finding of an arbitration board would need to receive at least as widespread publication as the initial charge. Such publication would require news media cooperation and some form of media access.

One model for such a process was the now defunct National News Council. This council, composed of a cross section of media critics and executives, was created to examine complaints about news reporting and to issue findings about these complaints. The goal was both to protect media from unwarranted criticism and to chastise media for improper reporting. While the goal was good, the process did not work well. Many major news organizations declined to participate and refused to cooperate with the council's investigations. Ideological differences among council members often prevented arrival at definitive conclusions, particularly on the many complaints that turned on matters of opinion rather than fact. In fact, a substantial number of the complaints received by the commission sprang from the ideological base of the far right. Finally, even when a clear conclusion was reached, it seldom received public notice. Large, mainstream media outlets ignored the council and its findings. This political polarization and the lack of support eventually led to the demise of the National News Council. Any successful libel arbitration program would need to

deal with problems of political ideology and receive media support and access to succeed. The
prospects are not good. As Bezanson, Cranberg,
and Soloski discovered, attitudes of arrogance and
defensiveness exist within the news media that
may well preclude any cooperation.

In 1988 the Libel Reform Project of the
Annenberg Washington Program of Northwestern
University produced a comprehensive libel reform
proposal complete with a model law. The proposal
draws on suggestions of both Haiman and the
Iowa Project. The model law would require a
plaintiff to ask for a retraction or right to reply and
would permit a suit only if that request was not
granted (the Haiman idea). Either side could ask
for a declaratory judgment that would in effect be
a finding about the truth or falsity of the disputed
communication (the Iowa Project idea). The losing
side would pay all litigation costs at this stage. If a
defamation suit were to go to trial, awards would be
limited to proven actual injury. While bills to enact
this model law have been introduced in a number of
states, strong news media opposition has prevented
passage of this legislation in any state.

One contribution to the present resentment
of news media toward defamation suits is their

costs. As some of the cases discussed in prior
chapters illustrate, even when a media defendant
wins, the cost of the litigation may be in the millions. These litigation costs make up an estimated
80 percent of the total cost of a defamation suit for
a media defendant. A losing plaintiff can face similar costs. It is, however, difficult to feel much
sympathy for media defendants when the news
media, waving the banner of freedom of the press,
doggedly resist sensible proposals for change such
as the Annenberg Washington Program model for
defamation law.

This problem of costs became the subject of a
special conference held in 1986 at the Gannett
Center for Media Studies at Columbia University.
Participants included media representatives, lawyers, and two famous defamation plaintiffs, Anthony Herbert and William Tavoulareas. The one
specific suggestion offered at the conference was a
call for expanded use of declaratory judgment for
media defendants. Obviously the cost of litigation
would be reduced if a trial court judge would
grant such a judgment early in the process in more
cases. While such a judgment would appear appropriate in a number of the cases discussed in
prior chapters, that judgment would not satisfy

the plaintiff. The *Conference Report* includes portions of the speech in which Colonel Herbert observed, "All I've been asking for 14 years is the right to face my accusers. All I want to do is get before a jury and let the jury hear what I have to say, let the jury look at the evidence." This statement indicates that Colonel Herbert, like most defamation plaintiffs, wants a definitive judgment about the truth or falsity of charges rather than money.

A number of news organizations have developed a self-help policy to deal with costs through filing counter-suits against defamation plaintiffs. These suits seek to recover litigation costs by charging malicious litigation. In some states the law allows this process to take place through the simple filing of a motion to recover costs. The idea is to make the plaintiff pay for filing a meritless complaint. These motions can sometimes be directed at both the plaintiff and the plaintiff's lawyer. While the obvious purpose of these actions is to solve the problem of litigation cost, widespread publication of the policy is intended to discourage defamation litigation. This approach solves some of the news media's problems but, like denying a right to reply, fails to give those who feel that they have been defamed an opportunity to present their case.

Defamation, like most difficult freedom of expression problems such as free press/fair trial, presents a conflict between competing values. On the one hand there is the tradition of unencumbered freedom of expression in the United States supported by the Constitutional guarantee of the First Amendment. On the other there is the commitment to the individual's right to privacy and the value we place on maintaining a good reputation. We agree with Shakespeare's famous lines from *Othello*:

> Who steals my purse steals trash. . . .
> But he that filches from me my good name
> Robs me of that which not enriches him
> And makes me poor indeed.

Subscribing to the sentiment, we often fail to notice that Shakespeare gave this line to Iago, who was embarked on a campaign of malicious defamation designed to destroy reputations. His defamations had tragic consequences. Shakespeare recognized the power and damage of such communication.

It is obvious that there is no simple or easy solution to the problem of defamation. Proposals such as those by Franklyn Haiman, the Iowa Project, and the Annenberg-Northwestern Libel Reform Project offer useful suggestions for change, but changes in the law can deal with only part of the problem. Attitudes toward and within the news media also need to be addressed. Greater tolerance for a diversity of opinion needs to be fostered. Such tolerance would preclude the use of defamation suits as a way to restrict the universe of public discourse to a single ideological view. For too many years the radical right, with massive financial resources at its disposal, has used defamation laws to punish the media and promote conformity to its ideology. Even though the basic ideology of the media is conservative, it is not conservative enough for these ideologues.

Arrogance within the news media also needs to be addressed. Those in control of mass media need to discover that there is nothing wrong with admitting error, correcting the public record, and apologizing. The vigorous resistance to the proposed sensible reform legislation apparently springs from an unwillingness to give up absolute control over the content of the news. However, a number of media critics such as Jerome Barron argue that real freedom of expression today depends upon expanded public access to the media. Freedom of the press should be the right of all Americans rather than just those who own the media. The result would surely be improved credibility and acceptance of the news media by the public, and everyone would win.

Annotated
Case List

Selected
Annotated
Bibliography

Annotated Case List

Many of the cases discussed in this book have produced recorded opinions by the judges who heard the case at trial or on appeal. These opinions present extended discussions by the judges of their understanding of defamation and their way of balancing the competing demands of freedom of expression and protection of reputation. Many of these opinions are written in a clear and lively manner, and all provide understanding at greater depth of the issues involved in defamation suits. Each opinion is identified by its own specific citation number, for example, 123 U.S. 456. The first number identifies the volume number of the published record in which the opinion appears, and the last number is the page number on which the opinion begins. The letters in the middle identify the series of volumes (e.g., *United States Reports*) of published opinions in which the case opinion appears. Most larger libraries carry these publications as do county law libraries.

Major Cases Discussed in This Book

Curtis Publishing Co. v. Butts; Associated Press v. Walker, **388 U.S. 130 (1967).** This pair of cases decided together expanded the concept of public official originally stated in the landmark *Times v. Sullivan* case to include well-known public figures such as a prominent football coach and a retired army general who had placed himself in the forefront of the antidesegregation battle. The opinion explores the rationale for requiring proof of a higher level of fault for public figures as well as public officials.

Gertz v. Robert Welch, Inc., **417 F.2d 801 (1971), 418 U.S. 323 (1974).** This landmark Supreme Court defamation decision provided a definition that still applies for the concept of public persons—namely persons who inject themselves into matters of public controversy in an attempt to influence the outcome. This opinion also spelled out when and under what circumstances different kinds of damages may be awarded. The first citation is to the court of appeals decision in this case.

Ginzburg v. Goldwater, **414 F.2d 324 (2d Circuit 1969), 396 U.S. 1049 (1970).** The first citation is to the opinion of the Second Circuit Court of Appeals that upheld the trial court jury's award in Senator Goldwater's defamation suit against Ralph Ginzburg and *fact* magazine. The second citation is to Justice Hugo Black's dissent when the Supreme Court of the United States refused to accept Ginzburg's appeal of that decision. An earlier version of the story of Barry Goldwater's suit against Ralph Ginzburg appeared in the *Free Speech Yearbook, 1983,* published by the Speech Communication Association.

Green v. Alton Telegraph, **438 N.E.2d 203 (1982).** This recorded opinion of the Illinois appeals court denies relief to the *Alton Telegraph.* The original trial court decision is reported in the Illinois records as No. 77-66 (Madison County, Illinois 1980).

Herbert v. Lando, **568 F.2d 974 (2d Circuit 1977), 441 U.S. 153 (1979), 596 F.Supp. 1178 (S.D.N.Y. 1984), 781 F.2d 298 (2d Circuit 1986).** These four citations record the long and checkered history of what are in effect two cases. The first two opinions by the circuit court and the Supreme Court of the United States first deny and then grant Herbert's lawyers the right to ask "state of mind" questions of those who prepared the broadcast about him. The second two citations concern the granting of summary judgment to CBS on the disputed statements in the broadcast.

Hutchinson v. Proxmire, **443 U.S. 111 (1979).** The Court's opinion comments on and refines the concept of public person developed in *Gertz v. Welch.* In addition it considers the nature and limits of privileged communication.

Ilya Wolston v. Reader's Digest Association, Inc., **443 U.S. 157 (1979).** This opinion by Justice William Rehnquist, like *Time v. Firestone,* further limited the concept of public person. In this case fifteen years' time made someone who might once have been a public figure a private person.

New York Times v. Sullivan, **376 U.S. 254 (1964).** This landmark opinion from which all later federal court opinions on defamation flow established guidelines and limitations on defamation suits based on the First Amendment guarantee of freedom of the press by establishing standards for fault that would need to be proven by public officials who sue for libel. The Alabama Supreme Court opinion in this case can be found in 273 Ala. 656, 144 So. 2d 25 (1962).

Paul, Chief of Police, Louisville v. Davis, **424 U.S. 693 (1976).** The majority opinion by Justice Rehnquist seems to grant unlimited and unqualified privilege to all law enforcement officials' communication that might be considered part of their official duties. A judgment against the police chief for the publication of knowing falsehoods was reversed.

Pring v. Penthouse Int'l., Ltd., **695 F.2d 438 (10th Circuit 1982).** A humorous short story about a mythical Miss Wyoming's sexual fantasies while performing in the Miss America Pageant led to a suit by a former Miss Wyoming and a $26.5 million jury award. The court of appeals decision cited here overturned the award by concluding that no reasonable reader could see the story as anything other than fiction and fantasy.

Rosenblatt v. Baer, **383 U.S. 75 (1966).** This case made it clear that the elected public official concept enunciated in *Times v. Sullivan* also included appointed public officials with limited power and authority.

Rosenbloom v. Metromedia, Inc., **403 U.S. 29 (1971).** In Justice Brennan's plurality opinion the Supreme Court of the United States stated that there was no real difference between private and public persons in news stories "of public or general concern," which in effect meant that all defamation plaintiffs would need to prove the reckless disregard or knowing falsehood level of fault.

St. Amant v. Thompson, **390 U.S. 727 (1968).** Justice Byron White's brief opinion for the Court offered by definition and example a clear explanation of the evidence needed to prove actual malice—the publication of reckless or knowing falsehoods.

Sharon v. Time, **599 F.Supp. 538 (S.D.N.Y. 1984).** This is the decision of the trial court not to grant *Time*'s request for a summary judgment and to allow the case to go to trial.

Tavoulareas v. Washington Post Co., **567 F.Supp. 651 (D.D.C. 1983); 759 F.2d 90 (D.C. Circuit 1985); 817 F.2d 762 (D.C. Circuit 1987).** The three opinions cited here deal with judicial review of the jury verdict against *The Washington Post*. The trial judge set aside the verdict, the court of appeals reinstated the verdict, and then the entire court of appeals once again set the original jury decision aside.

Time, Inc. v. Mary Alice Firestone, **424 U.S. 448 (1976).** The opinion written by Justice Rehnquist in this case reaffirmed the principle from *Gertz v. Welch* that public persons, no matter how well known, must voluntarily thrust themselves into a controversy. In addition, the opinion expanded the range of errors that might be considered negligent.

Westmoreland v. CBS, **10 Med.L.Rep. (BNA) 2417 (S.D.N.Y. 1984).** This is the case that was never decided because General Westmoreland withdrew his complaint before the trial concluded.

Other Important Related Cases

Alioto v. Cowles Communications, Inc., **430 F.Supp. 1363 (N.D.Cal. 1977).** Through a series of four trials over a period of eight years former San Francisco Major Alioto (a public official) finally won a $400,000 judgment against Cowles Communications for its publication of the charge that he had organized crime connections.

Jack Anderson v. Liberty Lobby, Inc., **477 U.S. 242 (1986).** In this case the Supreme Court of the United States addressed the issue of summary judgment in favor of a media defendant and ruled that a plaintiff must prove defamation with "convincing clarity" in order to bring a case to trial.

Beauharnais v. Illinois, **343 U.S. 250 (1952).** Through a group libel law (since repealed) the State of Illinois criminalized some forms of defamatory communication. This decision and opinion upheld the conviction and jailing of Beauharnais for the publication and distribution of a racist pamphlet.

Bose Corp. v. Consumers Union, **466 U.S. 485 (1984).** A critical evaluation of the Bose 901 speaker containing some minor factual errors led to a $115,000 damage award that was set aside when the first circuit court of appeals reviewed the evidence and found it insufficient. When Bose appealed, arguing that the court of appeals should not have reexamined the facts of the case, the Supreme Court of the United States upheld the decision of the court of appeals.

Brown & Williamson v. Jacobson, **835 F.2d 1119 (7th Circuit 1987).** A broadcast on WBBM-TV in Chicago falsely accusing Viceroy cigarettes of planning an ad campaign designed to persuade youngsters to smoke led to a $3.05 million judgment—the largest ever to be upheld by an appellate court opinion. The Supreme Court of the United States refused to hear the case.

Burnett v. National Enquirer, 7 **Med.L.Rep. (BNA) 1321 (Cal.Super.Ct. 1981); 144 Cal.App.3d 991 (1983).** Because of the fame of the parties involved, this is perhaps the most well-known defamation case. A jury awarded Carol Burnett $1.6 million for a short *Enquirer* report that had suggested her public drunkenness even though a retraction had been published. This award, later reduced to $800,000, was upheld on appeal.

Cantrell v. Forest City Pub. Co., **419 U.S. 245 (1974).** A fictionalized news story about Mrs. Margaret Cantrell that appeared in the *Cleveland Plain Dealer* led to a $60,000 jury award that was sustained in this opinion. The legal basis for this judgment, false light invasion of privacy, is similar to defamation.

Garrison v. Louisiana, **379 U.S. 64 (1964).** James Garrison, New Orleans District Attorney, was convicted of criminal defamation for statements he made in a press conference criticizing the work habits of New Orleans judges. While the trial court found that he had spoken with malicious intent, the Supreme Court of the United States reversed the conviction, ruling that such communication could not be criminalized.

Hustler Magazine v. Falwell, **485 U.S. 46 (1988).** A parody of a Compari ad that appeared in *Hustler* suggesting drunkenness and incest led Rev. Jerry Falwell to sue for libel, invasion of privacy, and intentional infliction of emotional distress. While finding against him on the first two claims, the jury awarded Falwell $200,000 for emotional distress. The Supreme Court opinion written by Chief Justice Rehnquist concluded that a public figure such as Falwell could not collect for emotional distress due to a parody that might be found offensive.

Keeton v. Hustler Magazine, **465 U.S. 770 (1984).** Kathy Keeton, Vice-Chairman of *Penthouse,* filed suit in New Hampshire for five items that appeared over a period of nine months in *Hustler.* The suit was filed in New Hampshire even though she was a resident of New York and *Hustler* was published in Ohio, because the standard one year statute of limitations had expired in all the other forty-nine states. Justice Rehnquist's opinion for the Court majority allowed the suit to be heard in spite of that fact that neither party had any real association with the state in which the case would be tried.

Miami Herald v. Tornillo, **418 U.S. 241 (1974).** The issue in this case was that of media access rather than defamation. Candidate for office Tornillo demanded the right to reply to a critical editorial as provided in Florida law. The Supreme Court of the United States rejected the idea of a statutory right to media access that had been argued vigorously by Tornillo's lawyer, Jerome Barron.

Ollman v. Evans, **750 F.2d 970 (D.C. Circuit 1984).** Eleven judges of the Fourth Circuit Court of Appeals hearing this case wrote a total of seven opinions. The case arose out of a syndicated newspaper column by Evans and Novak containing false statements about Marxist political science professor Bertell Ollman. Although the court ruled against Ollman, there was little agreement among the majority justices about the grounds for their decision.

Selected
Annotated Bibliography

The literature dealing with defamation is extensive. Any of the standard textbooks in media law devote several chapters to the subject and the news media's defenses against suits. The following is a selected list of nontext discussions of defamation.

Adler, Renata. *Reckless Disregard.* New York: Harper & Row, 1986. This volume contains the expanded reports on the Westmoreland and Sharon trials originally published in *The New Yorker* that attempt to make the case for the two generals that they could not make for themselves in court.

Barron, Jerome A. *Freedom of the Press for Whom?* Bloomington: Indiana University Press, 1973. Barron presents both philosophical and legal arguments for the premise that real freedom of speech is promoted by actions, including government regulation and law, that expand citizen access to both electronic and print media.

Bezanson, Randall P., Gilbert Cranberg, and John Soloski. *Libel Law and the Press.* New York: The Free Press, 1987. This is the first of what is anticipated to be a series of volumes growing out of the Iowa Libel Research Project.

Brill, Steven. "Inside the Jury Room at The Washington Post Libel Trial." *The American Lawyer,* Nov. 1982, 1, 89-94. Brill's interviews with members of the jury in the Tavoulareas libel suit as reported here show how difficult it is for the average person to understand the complexities of libel laws and apply them in a specific case.

Burton, Benjamin. *Fair Play.* New York: Harper & Row, 1988. The author of an internal CBS study "The Uncounted Enemy" describes the development of that report, the nature of its criticism of the documentary, and its distortion and misuse by General Westmoreland's supporters.

Forer, Louis G. *A Chilling Effect.* New York: W. W. Norton & Company, 1987. In this broad-ranging book the author, a lawyer and trial judge, considers over two hundred cases, many not usually discussed in the context of libel, and explores often overlooked issues such as parody and the infliction of emotional distress.

Haiman, Franklyn S. *Speech and Law in a Free Society.* Chicago: University of Chicago Press, 1981. Building upon his philosophical discussion of the nature and function of communication, Haiman offers two thoughtful chapters dealing with defamation and invasion of privacy.

Hayden, Trudy, and Jack Novik. *Your Right to Privacy.* New York: Avon Books, 1980. One of the series of "rights" volumes prepared by the American Civil Liberties Union, this volume explores the individual's right to be left alone and free of media attention.

Hopkins, W. Wat. *Actual Malice.* New York: Praeger Publishers, 1989. This volume focuses upon the concept of reckless or knowing falsehood—actual malice—as it existed prior to *New York Times v. Sullivan* and the way in which the definition of the concept has evolved in the twenty-five years since the Sullivan case.

Labunski, Richard. *Libel and the First Amendment.* New Brunswick, NJ: Transaction Books, 1987. Labunski explores the recent legal history of defamation litigation with particular attention to the difficult distinction between public and private persons.

Lawhorne, Clifton O. *Defamation and Public Officials.* Carbondale, IL: Southern Illinois University Press, 1971. Part of the New Horizons in Journalism series, the volume traces the development of defamation law in regard to public officials from the colonial period to *New York Times v. Sullivan.*

————. **The Supreme Court and Libel.** Carbondale, IL: Southern Illinois University Press, 1981. This update of the earlier volume traces public figure defamation from *Sullivan* to *Gertz.*

Littlewood, Thomas B. *Coals of Fire.* Carbondale, IL: Southern Illinois University Press, 1988. This study offers a detailed examination of the *Alton Telegraph* libel case and its implications.

Madsen, Axel. *60 Minutes.* New York: Dodd, Mead & Company, 1984. Chapter 14 in this general study of the "60 Minutes" program examines some of the program's legal problems including the Herbert and Westmoreland suits.

News Media and the Law
This quarterly journal published by The Re-

porters Committee for Freedom of the Press provides comprehensive coverage of current defamation litigation.

Rosenberg, Normal L. *Protecting the Best Men.* Chapel Hill, NC: University of North Carolina Press, 1986. Rosenberg's history of the laws of libel begins in colonial America and ends with the Sullivan case—the point at which Labunski's work begins.

Sanford, Bruce W. *Libel and Privacy.* New York: Harcourt Brace Jovanovich, 1985. This comprehensive reference volume provides detailed analyses of present law in every phase of defamation.

Smolla, Rodney A. *Suing the Press.* New York: Oxford University Press, 1986. This entertaining and informative volume by the director of the Annenberg-Northwestern Libel Reform Project discusses most of the well-known libel cases of the last twenty-five years.

Wallace, Mike, and Gary Paul Gates. *Close Encounters.* New York: William Morrow and Company, 1984. Mike Wallace's own story discusses Herbert, Westmoreland, and other CBS defamation cases from the point of view of a defendant.

Peter E. Kane is professor of communication and director of graduate studies in communication at the State University of New York, College at Brockport. He is chair of the Speech Communication Association's Freedom of Expression Commission, an associate editor of the SCA's *Free Speech Yearbook*, and he has served as editor of both *Free Speech* and the *Free Speech Yearbook*. His essays on freedom of expression appear in the seventy-fifth anniversary commemorative volumes for both the Eastern Communication Association and the Speech Communication Association. His book *Murder, Courts, and the Press: Issues in Free Press/Fair Trial* (Southern Illinois University Press, 1986) received the Eastern Communication Association's Everett Lee Hunt Award for distinguished scholarship.